# THE
# QUESTS

**by**

**VADA M. GIPSON**

ISBN: 1-4033-6424-9 (e-book)
ISBN: 1-4033-6425-7 (Paperback)

This book is printed on acid free paper.

1stBooks - rev. 09/13/02

# THE QUESTS

## Chapter One.

Mary came running down the stairs into the courtyard. Zipporah was right behind her. Mary went directly to Philip who had been pacing the earthen floor. Zipporah went to the outside door, saying, "I'm going for my husband." Watching her run by, Philip turned and said, "We heard the baby cry. Everything is all right…isn't it?"

Worry and fatigue from the long night showed in Mary's face as she looked up into Philip's eyes and said, "Son, you have another girl. She came about a month early and is very tiny, but fully developed. Hannah is not doing well. She's asking to see you."

He took off like an arrow to their chamber, taking the steps three at a time, his mother following on the run. "The midwife did everything she could to stop the bleeding, but it just keeps flowing. We made her as comfortable as we can."

He stopped at the door of their room and walked slowly to where Hannah was lying on her pallet. The newborn babe, oiled, rubbed with salt to toughen the skin, wrapped in strips of soft cloth to form straight limbs, and blankets, was lying beside her in the crook of her arm.

The sparsely furnished room was softly lighted by one pottery oil lamp near her bed. The three older children had been bedded in another room for this

1

night. The two sisters-in-law were disposing of the birthing supplies and material. The midwife was hovering over her patient, apprehension showing in the lines of her body.

Elias and Nathaniel, Philip's brothers who had been waiting with him, restlessly remained in the courtyard, according to tradition.

Philip dropped to his knees beside Hannah's bed on the floor. *She is so white*, he thought, *even in this pale light.*

Mary cleared her throat and quietly said, "Let's go tell the others." The sisters-in-law's sad eyes showed sympathy as they looked at Hannah and slowly turned away to go ahead of Mary to tell their husbands. The midwife stepped back and wrung her hands.

Before he could give utterance to words, Hannah breathed softly, "Philip..." She paused.

He waited.

"...I am dying."

Philip's chin dropped. With mouth opened and eyes staring wildly at his precious and devoted wife, he thought: *This can't be happening.* His eyes narrowed to slits and the tears began to flow down his cheeks. "Oh...merciful God, ...Hannah...don't say that...please don't even think about it..."

Hannah found the strength to place her finger on his lips. As he took her hand in his, she continued, "My life's blood...is draining from me. I want to... ask you something." She rested for a breath.

"What is it, dearest?" Terms of endearment were not unusual between Philip and Hannah.

"I honor you...father of my babies...head of household. I have a wish." Hannah rested again.

Tears choking his voice, Philip replied, "Whatever you want, if I can do it, I will."

Hannah's tired eyes looked into his. "You may marry again...." (It was not unusual for a widower to remarry very soon after the death of his wife.)

Philip jerked and dropped her hand. "No!"

She continued, "...I don't want...our girls...raised by a...stepmother. They're special."

"Yes, I know they are special, but I could never marry again. Never! You have no worry about them being raised by a stepmother. You are the only wife for me."

She closed her eyes and slowly opened them, then went on, "I want my parents...to take them...they will know...how to raise them...like they did me."

Philip raised her hand to his lips. Tears moistened the fingers as he caressed them. Choking, he answered softly, "If that's the way you want it, that's the way it will be. I love you, Hannah."

She took a breath and whispered, "I'm tired. I'll sleep now," and closed her eyes.

As she submitted to slumber, death drew a curtain over her countenance. At that moment, the oil in the lamp was gone and its flame flickered out. The room was softly bathed in the early light of dawn coming through the small window.

"Hannah. Hannah! HAN-NAH!!" Philip shouted.

At once the room was filled with all members of the family. Patting Hannah's face, trying to awaken her, he started to sob.

Zipporah, Hannah's mother, having returned with her husband, tearfully reached down and took the newborn babe, who had serenely slept through it all.

3

She buried her face in the blanket of the little one and cried, her husband hovering over them. Sarah and Elizabeth, the sisters-in-law, weeping, embraced each other, as did Elias and Nathaniel. Jacob, Philip's father, and Mary were on each side of Philip.

Hannah's eyelids had half-opened at the moment of death. As head of the household, it was Jacob's duty to close the eyes of the deceased. Reaching beyond Philip, Jacob gently pulled the eyelids down.

"We must beat the drum," Jacob said to no one in particular. The drumbeat was the message to the community of a death.

The funeral was typical of first century Judaic custom: before the sun set on the day of death. The women oiled, spiced, and wrapped the body in burial linen. The procession included the entire population of the village. The market places closed their doors for the afternoon. The local flute players donated their services. No professional mourners were hired—they were for the more affluent. Jacob, as village priest, was the main speaker, and other friends and relatives said a few words.

According to Judaic Law, for seven days after a death the house was unclean and no food could be prepared within it. Neighbors brought in food. Then followed the period of mourning, one to two months.

Philip took two months. He spent most of it on the pallet in his room. He would go to meals in the courtyard with the family, but he didn't have an appetite for food. He couldn't concentrate on table conversation—his mind would zigzag back to Hannah's deathbed and his guilt for having caused it.

The scene was burned in his mind forever. Even now, he could clearly hear the first cry of the newborn babe that pierced the quietness of this family compound in the seaside village of Bethsaida. He remembered the smiles that wreathed the faces of all who heard it and the conversation that took place when he said, "Praise the Lord! It finally made it!"

"Sounds like a healthy boy," Nathaniel had remarked, laughing.

Philip had been pacing the moonlit courtyard that night. The other male members of the household—his two younger brothers and their father—were keeping him company, but in a more relaxed manner. The animals in their pen in the courtyard were restless under the first full moon of spring. It had been a long birthing, and they were exhausted from lack of sleep.

Philip remembered that he seriously replied, "Boy or girl, I'm just glad it's here."

Jacob, his father, said as he stood up, "I'm going to bed...it won't be long till daylight. I'll wait to find out. Good night."

"Good night, Father," said the brothers. Philip had added, "Thanks for watching with me." Jacob left to go to his room in the family compound.

Philip remembered he murmured, "I just pray that Hannah will be healthy."

Elias, the elder of the two brothers, had said sympathetically, "She hasn't been strong, has she?"

He had hesitated before answering, "When the twins were born four years ago she was damaged, and... remember, she nearly died when our last child came. She had so much trouble... ...I swore that I'd never go into her again." He sobbed as he remembered

5

his next words, "I really love Hannah…so very much. I need her in my life. If anything happened to her because of me…I would never forgive myself."

"Come now, brother. Don't get down on yourself. With three girl babies, it was your duty to father a son," Nathaniel had exclaimed, teasingly.

"Not as important as preserving the life and health of my wife!" he had shot back. "It wasn't a duty when I did it. It was pure lust… …that longing in the night, and Hannah's beautiful body so near me." And he felt even worse, as he went over it in his mind.

After a moment of embarrassed silence Elias had said, "We've been blessed with the wives that Father arranged for us."

"It helps to have the village priest for a father," Nathaniel had interjected.

Elias had continued, "I know that I could not want a better one than my Sarah. She helps Mother around the house and garden; she's a good mother to our little one…."

"She waits on you like a slave," Nathaniel had added.

"Yes, I admit that I enjoy having her attention. But your wife takes good care of you, too, so don't be envious of me."

"Ah, my little Elizabeth is the light of my life. I had my eye on her for a long time before Father started shopping for me." He had hesitated, then continued more seriously, "I'm like Philip…I would not want to lose her."

Philip remembered that he said, "When Father told me that he had arranged for Hannah to be my wife, I

6

was apprehensive. But the first time I saw her, and knew I would have her, it excited me."

Nathaniel had chuckled and said, "Yes, I remember!"

It pained Philip to remember that as he continued, "It still does. But she has more than just a physical attraction…she is intelligent, caring, can think and reason. I can talk to her almost like a man. I've learned to really love and depend on her."

"All that and she reads and writes, too." interjected Elias.

"Yes, being an only child, her father taught her, and she's planning to teach our girls. She comes from a line of prophets …through her mother's side. The twins are showing signs that they have inherited the gift…. Here comes someone."

Philip's mind snapped back to the present, but it would then go through the death scene, down to the finest detail. Desperately he would try to keep Hannah from dying, he wanted to cling to her with his love. Little did he realize that his feeling of guilt had started to gnaw deeper and deeper within his being.

## Chapter Two

"How are you doing, son?" Jacob tenderly asked Philip, while at the dining table one afternoon after the mourning period,

"Not too well, Father. I know it has been two months but it seems like yesterday that I lost her."

To allow him to grieve, others had filled in for him: Jacob arranged for the grave; Elias, who usually went with Nathaniel on their fishing boat, went to the synagogue as the teacher.

Hannah's mother had kept the new baby, but the older girls remained in Jacob's home. In a household with extended family such as Jacob's, all the work, income, and expenses were shared, including caring for the children. But each child had a primary caregiver, so Grandmother Mary looked after the two-year-old, while Aunt Elizabeth, who had no children yet, took care of the four-year-old twins.

Philip's promise to let Hannah's parents raise the girls constantly came to mind, and he would feel more and more guilty of neglecting his word. Then he would remember the reason: she didn't want them raised by a stepmother. *Well, he had no intention of marrying again.* So he took no action to comply with her dying wish.

Philip would have no trouble finding another wife, if he chose to marry again. Twenty-seven years old, he had long, black hair and beard, a tanned fair complexion and blue eyes, as did all the male members of Jacob's family. Philip was the tallest by about an inch—he stood five feet, 11 inches. His mother, Sarah, and his two sisters, one older than he was and one younger than Nathaniel, all had deep brown eyes, as well as dark hair. The sisters were both married, living with husbands in their parents' homes.

Jacob's household was a member of the Holy Ones, called the "Essene Sect" by outsiders. The high priests at the temple in Jerusalem were men who had been put in office by kings and rulers; therefore, the Holy Ones considered them illegitimate. When this first happened (about 150 years before), the true priests, the descendants of Zadok (High Priest for King Solomon), fled Jerusalem and maintained their own religion. The Holy Ones were outstanding wherever they went because of the pure white garments they wore. Jacob and his household were no exception.

Now, Jacob was saying, "You'll feel better if you get on with your life, don't you agree? Nathaniel is anxious to get Elias back to the nets with him."

"All right, Father, I'll go to the synagogue with you tomorrow morning and try to put this behind me."

When morning came, Philip took up his duties as a teacher at the synagogue. Elias went back to the boat with Nathaniel.

The Torah was taught verbally. The keynote of Judaism, the Shema, was followed to the letter: "Hear, O Israel: The Lord our God is one Lord; and you shall love the Lord your God with all your heart, and with all your soul, and with all your might. And these

9

words which I command you this day shall be upon your heart; and you shall teach them diligently to your children, and shall talk of them when you sit in your house, and when you walk by the way, and when you lie down, and when you rise."

Fathers were responsible for teaching their sons, starting while they were yet toddlers. When the boys reached the age of five, they were brought at dawn to the synagogue where their formal education continued. For five years, six days a week, the little ones sat at the teacher's feet, repeating sounds and words, memorizing the written laws of their people. Their school day ended at about midday. When a child reached the age of ten, he was ready for the advanced school, which taught the oral laws as well as the written ones. Jacob taught those students. Not all boys went.

Every man had to make a living. The boys learned their father's trade or were apprenticed to someone else. Jacob and Philip were public letter writers. A sharpened reed was the badge of their craft. They wore it over their ear.

Women taught the girls, and they had much to learn. The men may have plowed the garden or field for them in the spring, but the raising of crops was usually women's work. They grew grain, cucumbers, melons, leeks, onions, garlic, peas and beans. They ground their own flour with either a rotary mill or a grinding stone. Mary and her daughters-in-law used the rotary mill, which was more efficient.

Much of their work took place in the courtyard where stood a large oven made of stone in which was baked their daily bread. They raised goats and sheep for milk, meat and wool, and chickens for meat and eggs. They spun the wool and made their own garments. The village women bartered for produce they didn't grow themselves.

Two meals were prepared each day, except on the Sabbath, which were made ready the day before. The first meal was a light one, eaten between mid-morning to midday. Supper was substantial. Eggs, cheese or fish were served along with vegetables, bread and butter, and fruit and perhaps watered wine. Meat was eaten on special occasions and festivals. The table was barely raised off the earthen floor, and the diners sat on the ground.

It wasn't long before Philip realized that his heart wasn't in his teaching. The guilt he felt about Hannah's death was paralyzing him. He longed to remove himself from this scene—to start anew somewhere else. *But, where?* Casting about in his mind, he remembered the Brotherhood at Qumran. The more he thought about it, the more he wanted to go there and try living the life of the more austere members of his sect. He calculated it was about four days journey south. From visitors, he knew it was located in the wilderness west of Lake Asphaltitis. Being a loyal son, he would not feel right unless he obtained his father's permission. And how was he going to do that?

As Jacob and Philip were walking together from the synagogue to their home soon thereafter, Philip said, "Father," then hesitated.

"What is it, my son?"

"It's been two weeks since I returned to the classroom."

"Yes. How are you doing?"

"I'm finding it impossible to keep my mind on the teachings."

"Perhaps you're expecting too much too soon. You've always been a perfectionist. Give yourself more time."

"I feel paralyzed. I'm not helping those children learn anything, and I'm not helping myself."

"What can I say, Philip?"

"I have reached the point where I feel I must make a change in my life."

Jacob took him by the arm to stop him, looked him in the eye, and asked, "A change? What do you mean? What kind of change?"

"With your permission, I would like to... ...I wish to go to the Brotherhood at Qumran for awhile."

"Qumran!" Eyes bulging as he stared at Philip. "They are very strict. You wouldn't have the comforts there that we have here."

"I know." Philip started the walk again. "Visitors at the synagogue have told me about their routine. It's not for comfort that I'd be going. I need to get away from memories of Hannah." Philip stopped walking and turned to look at his father, tears welling in his eyes. "Everywhere I look, I expect to see her, and then the realization of her death hits me again."

After a moment of silence, they took up their pace. Jacob slowly said, "I suppose I shouldn't admit this to you, Philip, but I'm a little envious that you are free...and want to go. I wanted to, also, when I was young."

"You wanted to go?" They hesitated in their walking before Philip continued, "That is a surprise!"

"Yes, it's true. An earthquake destroyed the place before I was born, about sixty years ago, and Qumran was deserted. About thirty years ago, a remnant that had fled to Damascus returned to rebuild it. Many of the sons of priests that I knew were going to help."

"What happened that you didn't?"

"I was already betrothed to your mother, and it would have been a hardship for her. I was helping my father here in the village, just as you're helping me." He hesitated and thoughtfully added, "Perhaps I just didn't have the courage to do what you want to do."

Smiling for the first time in a long while, Philip said, "It pleases me, and lifts my spirits, to know that you also wanted to go."

Together they reviewed the events that happened to cause the priests to leave Jerusalem: The Maccabean revolt took place about two hundred years before, brought about by the worship of foreign gods being forced on the people by Seleucid rulers. The high priest instigated the revolt, and his three sons, especially Judas, defeated all adversaries. Then the office of high priest was combined with that of ruler of the country.

Philip said, "With that kind of power soon came corruption of the temple."

"You're right. The First John Hyrcanus, a grandson, succeeded Mattathias, the priest who started the revolt. When John died, he left the throne to his wife! His first-born son, Aristobulus, put his mother in a dungeon where she starved…"

"And he was a priest?"

"That's not all…he put three brothers in prison, and had his fourth brother murdered. He didn't live long, but as far as I know, died of natural causes."

"Then what happened?"

"One of the jailed brothers, Alexander Janneus, killed one of the two remaining brothers. He was a wicked priest. He openly defiled the temple with foreign gods and ways that had started the revolt in the first place. A riot by priests at a celebration of the Feast of the Tabernacles started a rebellion that cost thousands of lives and lasted nine or ten years."

"That was when the priests fled to Qumran?"

"Yes. Qumran was an old fort that had been occupied now and then for hundreds of years."

"How come your grandfather was not one of them?"

"Every twenty-four weeks the priests throughout the land served a week at the Holy Temple in Jerusalem. It was not the week for my grandfather to be there. He continued on here as village priest, teaching the Torah and unwritten laws, as he had been doing, but he no longer went to the temple."

"But we wear the white robes of the Holy Ones. How did we know to do this?"

"The Rules of Discipline from Qumran were studied by every village priest. It must have taken many months to a year for everyone to know of them. Most priests chose to be loyal to the imposter, but our ancestor remained true to his principles."

"Then I am completing the cycle of events that began in Great-Grandfather's day."

"That's right. You are."

They walked a few paces in silence. Philip said, "I was thinking that Elias can take my place at the synagogue. He's a natural teacher and has the temperament for it. Nathaniel can either hire someone to take his place on the boat or get a new partner. Can't he?"

"Yes. We will work it out somehow." Hesitating a moment, he asked, "When do you plan to leave?"

"After the Sabbath. I'll have Nathaniel take me to the south end of the Sea of Galilee on his boat, and I'll follow the Jordan to Lake Asphaltitis."

"I see that you have been giving this a lot of thought," Jacob responded as they reached the door into the courtyard of their home.

Philip stopped and embraced his father. "I feel so much better, Father, after having talked to you. Thank you for blessing my plan. I'm looking forward to getting my journey started."

## Chapter Three

Nathaniel's fishing was done during the night with a lantern to attract the fish. The well-traveled road was about twelve miles across the lake. He would leave earlier than usual this trip and put Philip on land before dark.

Philip spent the morning of the first day of the week preparing his bags of food for the journey, and saying goodbye to friends and family. It was a tearful farewell.

The main thoroughfare between the Sea of Galilee and Jerusalem started on the west side of the Jordan. It crossed to the east of the winding, twisting river below the mouth of River Yarmuk that came in from the east. The stream was crossed again near Jericho.

After walking as far as he could before dark, Philip found a spot near the river where other travelers had stopped for the night. He thought: *there will be safety in numbers*. He washed in the river, prayed over his food and ate from the rations he had brought. Unrolling his goatskin pallet, he wondered if he could escape the nightly visions of Hannah. He lay on his bed, and waited for sleep to come. Looking up through the branches of trees, he could see the stars. His mind went back to his youth when he was a helper on a fishing boat. He loved being out under the open sky, smelling the water, and hearing the seagulls. What carefree days they were!

A night bird made its call. Was it an owl? He realized that he had missed being out in God's creation—the small wild animals that were not too fearful of man, and the birds. Everyday of the week he had gone to and from the synagogue, not aware of the sights and sounds of nature. He was going to enjoy this trip. But as soon as conscious thought gave way to the unconscious, Hannah was there, dying in his arms. And he knew it was because of his actions.

At dawn he was up and on his way. A few travelers kept Philip company for a while, others passed him by. Most of the people were on foot, but a few traveled by litter or cart. Afternoons were too hot to travel, so everyone sought shady spots in which to rest. Philip enjoyed the afternoon rests especially because the wild life came within view. A big rabbit with long ears came close enough that he could have caught it, if he had wanted to. Another afternoon as he was watching the sky, a scene he had never witnessed before thrilled him: a golden eagle swooped down, picked up a rodent in her giant claws and flew off to a big nest high in a tree nearby.

As Philip neared the northern end of Lake Asphaltitis, also known as the Dead Sea, he spotted the tower of the building at Qumran. It was located to his right, on a plateau set back from the lake with deep ravines on each side. Behind it were higher bluffs, and the Wilderness of Judea that lay east of Jerusalem and Bethlehem. *It is so arid,* he mused, *and look at that blue haze hanging over the lake! I have heard the salt content in the water is so high that nothing can sink.*

*What is that odor, and what is causing this peculiar pressure in my ears?* (He couldn't know that it was 1,300 feet below sea level—twice that of the Sea of Galilee.) On his left, across the lake, were the cliffs of Moab.

The night before had been spent with members of his sect in Jericho. It was now about midday. After leaving the road to Jericho, he was alone. Not one other traveler was on the road.

He went to the river, bathed, found a shady spot, prayed, and ate his midday meal of bread, cheese, dates and raisins. Then he rested. The sun was lower in the west when he resumed his trek.

Philip found a walking staff and was glad to have it to help him with the walk up the trail of the ravine. Periodic flooding over the ages had laid down layers of limestone. The wilderness range had pockets of chalk. Where he was, the chalk had washed down into the ravines. *I am walking through chalk, he realized. The fine powder is caking between my feet and sandals.*

Very little vegetation broke the monotony of the sandstone walls. An occasional lizard darted for cover.

Facing the late afternoon sun, the climb was taking longer than expected. Periodically stopping to rest, Philip would turn and view the enlarging scene below. He could look down on hawks lazily searching for food. The geography of the green Jordan Valley contrasted against the blueness of the lake and almost cloudless sky and the beige-colored, barren cliffs of Moab bordering the far shore of the lake. The haze from the water softened their contours, rendering them almost featureless.

Finally reaching the top Philip found himself beyond the compound. Turning to approach the buildings, one of his many thoughts was thankfulness that the sun, at last, was on his back. The walled structures occupied about two acres. He estimated the main edifice measured approximately 100 feet by 125. The construction appeared to be of roughly cut stone blocks, mortared with mud. The most prominent feature of the rectangle was the lookout tower located on his left. He mused: *Is my approach being watched?*

He was happy to find the plateau was almost level with a very gentle eastward slope. He was following an aqueduct that went through the nearest corner of the wall. He turned to see where it came from. It appeared to terminate below a cliff that may have had a waterfall in rainy weather. Philip remembered having heard of the many baths taken by the brotherhood. *This must be the source of their water,* he reasoned. *I wonder how it is stored.*

"Shalom! Welcome, brother," was shouted by a white-robed man approaching Philip. "We've been expecting you! Come in and rest."

# Chapter 4

"Thank you. I am Philip of Bethsaida. May I ask your name?"

"Elihu. I serve in the watchtower. You came into view this morning while on the path from Jericho."

"That's when I spotted the tower and knew where to go."

Philip was guided through a gate in the wall, below the tower. Inside was a short corridor, with a wall on the right and buildings on the left and across the end. He saw an opening in the wall on the right that would have led them into a sheep pen, surrounded with walls and a building. Instead, they entered the room on the left, turned to their left, went through a storeroom below the lookout tower, and into a large kitchen. Philip welcomed the coolness the rock walls provided the interior of the buildings. He noticed plaster on the interior walls; the floor was paved with pebbles. Located on an outside wall was an oven, its flue going through the wall behind it.

"Brother, this is Philip of Bethsaida. He will be eating in the kitchen this evening. Philip, Brother Jesse will be in charge until you talk with the Examiner after supper."

"Shalom. Welcome to Qumran, Philip. Put your traveling bag in that corner. You will be sitting next to it when you eat."

"Thank you. Shalom, peace to you."

"You may wash in the basin over here."

Philip helped Jesse and his assistants with the final preparation for supper. It consisted of bread, cheese, vegetables, dates and raisins. Fifteen men ate together in the kitchen. The one among them who had been there the longest, almost two years, said the blessing before eating. Jesse ate with the other men in the dining hall.

Sparse conversation while eating revealed to Philip that he was among visitors to the compound and those who were serving a newcomer's probation before being fully accepted into the Covenant. Several were in their first year and had not yet received their loincloth, white linen robe and small ax. The others, dressed in white robes, were in the one-year period between preparatory and full membership. They were allowed in the daily bath rituals, but could not join with full members at mealtime.

After eating, Philip helped the kitchen crew to wash and ready the room for the next day.

When he relaxed he realized that he was very tired. Then Jesse came for him. He picked up his belongings and was led to the dining hall. There he met Brother Aaron, the Examiner, who invited Philip to sit across the table from him. The room was long and narrow, with four small windows and an outside door. He now knew that this was the east side of the rectangle. A long table ran down through the center, with benches on each side. It would accommodate sixty persons, he guessed. Jesse had left a lighted oil lamp, although dusk had not yet fallen.

"Tell me about yourself, Philip."

Philip related that he was a "Son of Zadok," raised by the Rules of Discipline from the Covenant at Qumran.

"Have you come to join us, or is this a sojourn?"

"I really don't know. My wife died in childbirth about three months ago...I have four daughters. I teach at the synagogue, but couldn't keep my thoughts on my work. I've come here on a quest for peace of mind, to see if this life's for me."

"Your honesty shows your upbringing in our tradition. As you know, we keep no secrets here. Even though you have been reared by our rules, it was not under our scrutiny. Therefore, you will be given the year's probation that we allow all candidates. You will have plenty of time, and no pressure from us, to decide if you wish to make this place your home. Meanwhile, tomorrow you will be given the Rules of Discipline to read for yourself. They are not to be broken; for that reason we must ask that you not wear your white robe here. You will be given one of another color.

Philip swallowed. This was something he had not considered.

Aaron paused, seeing Philip's reaction, continued, "After a year, and you have proved to yourself and us that you want to continue as a neophyte, you will get it back."

Aaron hesitated, allowing Philip to comprehend. He continued, "We are a self-sustaining community, as you know, and everyone has a job to do. Right now we are in need of a scribe."

"A scribe?"

"You do write, don't you?"

"Oh! Yes."

"We provide scrolls of scripture to the synagogues throughout Judea and wherever Judaism is taught. That's one way we can be sure of the purity of the texts. Tomorrow, after morning prayer, you will go to the scriptorium and tell Brother Joseph that you will write what he reads."

"Someone will direct me as to where it is?"

"Yes. I'll take you to your cave now. Brother John is also a scribe. You will be sharing a cave with him and two or three others."

Philip exclaimed to himself, *a cave! So that's where they sleep!*

Although darkness had not fallen, Aaron picked up the lamp, and led Philip out of the compound to the edge of the plateau. A path led down the bank to two big caves. They by-passed the first one and went on to the second. Upon entering the cave, Aaron said, "Brothers, this is Philip, a Zadokite from Bethsaida. He will be sleeping in this cave."

A rustling sound emanated from within, indicating the movement of several bodies to take a look at Philip.

"Brother John, he is going to join you in the scriptorium. He needs a clean candidate's robe, and to be shown where to go. Will you take care of him?"

John rose to his feet. "All right, Brother Aaron. Shalom, Philip. Welcome to our cave."

"It's refreshingly cool in here." His eyes adjusted to the dim light. Philip and John exchanged exploratory looks at each other. Barely able to make out John's features, he wondered if John were as curious about him as Philip was to get a good look at

23

John. They were about the same age, bearded, with long dark hair. But there was an intensity in his very dark eyes that captured Philip's attention. Philip sensed from this brief scrutiny that cave-mate John was somebody very special. *Why*, he wondered, *was the Prophet Elijah coming into my mind?*

John said, "I shall go for your robe now so you will have it for tomorrow morning. We maintain silence from the time we get up until prayer time."

"Thank you, John," Aaron said. "Good night. Rest well, Philip."

"Good night, Brother Aaron," the men chorused together.

Philip found a place to put his belongings, and took out his pallet on which to sleep, being watched by the men. He removed his white robe, not knowing when he would again put it on. Folding it, his thoughts turned to the length of time that he had been wearing a white robe—ever since his thirteenth birthday. He had accepted it at his bar mitzvah, the rite of passage to manhood, never expecting to consent if asked to wear another color.

He sat on his goatskin pallet. He was glad he had brought it along. It gave him a sense of home. He took off his sandals, rubbing his feet to dislodge the chalk and dust that were still caked between his toes and in the crevices of the skin.

A voice said, "If you want to bathe your feet, there's a basin with some water in it by the opening."

"Thank you. That would feel good."

His tired body resisted the desire to get up and go bathe his feet, but he knew it would feel refreshing. Besides, it would be in bad taste to turn down the courtesy of concern, for they knew he was tired. He rose to his feet, walked over by the basin, put one foot in and then the other. It did feel good—it felt wonderful.

The men started asking him questions about himself, and sharing their own stories. The one nearest to him said, "You may not remember me, but I ate with you in the kitchen tonight. My name is Samuel. I am also a first year candidate. The others in our cave are full members, but John is the only scribe. He wears his white robe while he works. We wear what we call our work robes. When we come in for meals, the full members and those who have met the requirements after a year bathe in the flowing water and put on their white robes."

"What do candidates do? They need to bathe, too."

"We have basins and jars of water with which to wash ourselves. About every other day I go down to the river after supper, especially during hot weather, and have a refreshing bath."

"This countryside is so dry…where does the water come from?"

"During the rainy season water is channeled into deep cisterns in the compound. It is used very frugally, and the waste water is diverted to another cistern to water the stock."

"What kind of work do you do?"

"I am a potter. See those jars down there, lining the end?"

Philip looked where he indicated and saw for the first time many tall jars with lids along the wall of the cave. "Yes."

"I make those jars. The manuscripts are stored in them until a synagogue or priests take what they want. I also make dishes and basins, but my primary product is the tall jar with lid."

As he sat down to dry his feet, Philip asked, "What other jobs are there?"

"Most of the residents work in the gardens. They are located in a fresh water spring-fed valley south of the compound. Everything is grown there ...wheat for our flour, vegetables and fruit. Then we have donkeys, sheep and goats and chickens, so someone has charge of the animals. Inside the compound is the baker who grinds the flour and bakes the bread, the people who work in the kitchen take care of the surplus from the garden as well as prepare the two meals each day, and loom workers who make our robes. Also tanners who prepare the leather for the scrolls and other needs."

The sound of John's approach interrupted the conversation. "Here is your robe, Philip."

"Thank you, John." Philip took the robe. It felt like heavy linen fabric. It looked blue in the dim light of the cave. He placed it with his belongings and lay down on his bed.

He had been a little anxious about his reception by the members at Qumran, and his own reaction, but by the time he was ready to go to sleep, the anxieties gave way to his fatigue. The friendliness of his cave brothers caused him to relax. Although he probably wouldn't know them by their faces tomorrow, except John, it now being too dark to distinguish features, he felt accepted by them. As he drifted off to sleep, he had the sensation that he was still trudging up that chalky ravine. The nightly dreams of Hannah would not come until just before awakening the next morning.

# Chapter Five

Philip was pulled from his dream by the feeling of movement about him. The light of dawn had seeped gently into the cave. He knew the group had to assemble to be in prayer as the sun came up, but rising that morning was not easy. The hour before sunrise was always a special time for him, and getting out of bed to enjoy it had become a life-long habit, but this one took effort.

The other men in the cave were putting on their robes and leaving the cave. Donning his new robe, Philip was interested to see what colors the others would be wearing.

He and Samuel followed John up the path to the plateau. As soon as they left their cave, the sound of men praying could be heard. They were in the open area, east of the walled compound, facing the sunrise. Philip was surprised to see, off to one side, four or five women and a few young children. *I thought this place was for men only.* He made a mental note to make inquiry about them. The sound of everyone praying aloud reduced self-consciousness, so Philip joined in a loud voice, "Oh, Jehovah, hear my prayer!"

The praying lasted until the orb was full above the horizon. John said, "I'll show you the scriptorium now," as he strode off toward the compound. Everyone else was heading for his task.

"Tell me about the women and children...I didn't know they were allowed to come here."

"The Manual of Discipline allows for women and children. Most of them are visitors...sisters or widows. Sometimes they come for healings."

"Healings?"

"Yes. Our brotherhood is well-known for healings that have occurred here."

"I didn't know that. Are any of these women married to someone here?"

"They may be. If they're married to one of the men, the family must keep to themselves."

"What work do they perform?"

"If the women are able, they help in the fields or with the animals. They fix their own food, and stay in a tent, if they have one, or in the cave for women. The boys attend classes that are taught by the priests here."

John and Philip entered the same door that Aaron had taken him through the night before. They retraced the corridor Jesse had used to bring him from the kitchen, except they didn't go as far as the kitchen.

The scriptorium was a large room, long and narrow, with plastered individual writing tables and benches that would accommodate twelve scribes. The room was completely inside the compound, but it had light through windows that opened to the interior courtyard on one side and the corridor to the kitchen on the other. Reeds and terra cotta inkwells were on each table. Scrolls of leather and papyrus were on shelves across the end of the room. On the floor were some of Samuel's jars.

John and Philip were the first to arrive. Soon two more men came. John introduced Philip to Joseph, whom Philip had expected to meet, and Simon.

"Shalom, Philip," Joseph said. "You will be my scribe. I read and you write. Simon and John have been working together. At this time of year we are short of scribes, so I have had to do my own reading and writing. I'm working on the Book of Isaiah."

"Where shall I sit?"

"Simon and John will be at the far end of the room, so we will stay at this end." Joseph handed him a piece of leather, which he placed on the writing table. He knew it would be stitched to a scroll when finished. Joseph said, "We mark the margins first, and then the lines. The dimensions for each page are etched on your table."

Philip found the markings on his table, took a straight piece of wood, dipped a reed in the inkwell, and marked the margins. Turning the wood horizontally, he spaced lines to match those of the guide.

"Well done. I will read a few words, and you take your time in writing them. If you need any repeated, just say so. Above all else we want accuracy, and a legible script. When we have finished a section, you will read back to me what you have written, and I will follow on my copy." The drone of Simon reading to John had already begun.

Philip had mixed emotions about working on the Book of the Prophet Isaiah. It was a difficult book for him to study, and he seemed to shy away from it. Perhaps the Lord was giving it to him now as an opportunity to really study it.

So the morning passed. Joseph reading, Philip writing. Philip reading back that which he had written. During mid-morning the smell of freshly baked bread permeated the room. It was enough to give Philip an appetite.

About five hours after sunrise was time for the first of their two meals. The men from the gardens and fields and all over the compound were gathering to take their baths, change to their white robes, pray, and eat their food.

As Philip arose from the bench, he seemed to be permanently bent in a sitting position. He wasn't in the habit of staying in one position for such a long period of time. He went to the kitchen, washed in a basin, and after a prayer for blessing the food, ate with the group in the kitchen.

After the meal, the men in white changed to their work robes and returned to their duties. The afternoon was a repeat of the morning, with the men coming in, bathing, changing, prayer for the blessing, and eating. Philip again experienced stiffness in his lower body as he stood to go to the kitchen. During the meal he noticed that no one spoke at the dining table until after the prayer of blessing, and then very little was said. There was no casual conversation and no one visited with his seatmate. What was said was in a voice loud enough so everyone could hear and anyone could respond.

The next day would be the Sabbath. Before Philip left the scriptorium Joseph handed him a scroll from the shelf and said, "Here is a Manual of Discipline for you to study. You may leave it in here, if you wish, and study it after supper or tomorrow. But you will need to know what is in it."

"All right. I'll leave it here and come back after supper to start reading it."

"We will have assembly tomorrow after the morning prayer. We fast until after sundown; our food will have been prepared and the tables set by sunset today. No one does any manual labor on the Sabbath. We do not even relieve ourselves, if at all possible."

Philip thought, *I shall be careful how much liquid I consume.*

After the evening meal, it still being light, Philip went back into the scriptorium to start reading the Manual of Discipline. He was curious to read the document for himself. His grandfather had read a copy, but had to pass it on to the next village priest. So Philip's knowledge was what had been handed down from the study his grandfather had made of it. One of the few differences he found had to do with the length of probation time candidates were given—it was three years in his home group, and two years here.

Philip read that the members called themselves "the Penitents of Israel," "the elect," or "members of the new covenant." They repudiated the Jerusalem priesthood and withdrew from there to the desert. They studied the laws of Moses, were obedient to God's will and kept His covenant. Separation from evil and evildoers was the basic concept of the community.

Philip learned from the writings of a thoroughly developed doctrine of the Adversary and of angels. This was something more than he had studied in the books at his home synagogue. It sometimes referred to the "Sons of Light" versus the "Sons of Darkness." A sense of living in the end times prevailed throughout the writings. The final punishment was to be by fire; the final blessing of those living in purity at Qumran was earthly and materialistic.

The Examiner, or Superintendent, maintained rigid discipline. The group was made up of priests and laymen. The priests, who were called "the sons of Zadok," had authority, but not exclusively. The Chief Priest was the highest official, then the Examiner. A body of fifteen men, called the Many, was responsible for the faith and life of the community.

Sometime after being accepted, a new member turned all his property over to the community and had all things in common. Altar sacrifices were very limited; spiritual sacrifices were stressed. Ritual washing partly took the place of the sacrificial system.

The light was fading, so Philip decided to quit reading for the day. As he rose to place the scroll on the shelf from which Joseph had taken it, he realized that he was really very stiff—from having been seated so long, or so he thought. He was able to get straightened up and walked to his cave without trouble.

The cave mates were already on their pallets, and some sleeping. Philip quietly went to his bed, removed his robe and sandals and lay down. As he reviewed the events of the day, thoughts of Hannah kept getting in the way. Then his mind would go back to her deathbed, and his terrible guilt. *I should have expected this haunting punishment* he thought as he drifted off to sleep.

## Chapter Six

Dawn came very soon, or so it seemed. Philip was tired. The night's rest didn't seem to be enough. When it came to getting up, he had trouble making his knees support his weight. *What is happening to me?* Once he was upright, he had no trouble walking. He joined the group for Morning Prayer, and went to the room where the Examiner, Brother Aaron, interviewed him for the assembly. He waited to be the last to sit down, because the seating order was very important in this community.

The High Priest took his place at the center of a platform at the end of the room, assisted by two priests. Brother Aaron was one. After the group sang two psalms, the first priest read scripture from Leviticus. Philip guessed that they were reading the five books of Moses during the year, a portion each Sabbath. The High Priest asked for commentary on the reading. First one person and then another would express their thoughts to amplify the passage. Philip was enthralled with these intellectual discourses. His father conducted a similar forum for commentary on the scriptures, but Philip had never been exposed to the thoughts and ideas of learned men such as these.

Aaron then read scripture from Isaiah—a passage Philip had copied just the day before which included:

"A voice cries, 'in the wilderness prepare the way of the Lord, make straight in the desert a roadway for our God.'"

Commentary was invited. A member of the community stood and said, "It is my belief that this...our...group is preparing the way of the Lord...we are in the wilderness, we are separated from the unrighteous. We are here to receive instruction, and the writings of our Teacher of Righteousness has provided them."

Another member stood and said, "It's my belief that the 'wilderness' in this passage is our own searching. The 'voice' is from our inner self, and 'the straight roadway in the desert' means to clear away all the interference from totally serving our God."

Philip noticed that his cave-mate, John, waited until the speaker was finished and seated, then arose and said, "It is my belief that we will never reach the unrighteous as long as we remain in seclusion here in this compound. We must leave here and preach to men where they are, and where we find them. 'The way' is not the searching of Moses' Law, but to prepare the people for the Messiah by telling them of the importance of the Law in all of life. We need to be the voices!" And then he sat down.

Silence.

Philip was thrilled with this exchange of viewpoints. He had the feeling that John's view had gone beyond the accepted versions. Why else the silence?

Another man, wearing a colored robe, tentatively rose to his feet. Philip recognized him as being one of his meal-mates in the kitchen. His long hair and beard were light brown, and his eyes were blue. His skin was tanned, but one could see that it was fair. He said softly, "I am a visitor, but may I join this discussion?" Philip sensed there was something about this man that was different—a quality that vibrated beyond sight and sound.

The Chief Priest said, "Please tell us your name and where you are from."

"I am Y'shua from Galilee."

As he said this, Philip felt a thrill go through him and wondered *what is it about this man that gives me a feeling of excitement.*

"Go ahead, Y'shua."

"I give you a parable: A tradesman has a new product. It is a new idea…a concept that requires different thinking for it to be accepted. His potential customers are stiff-necked people set in their ways. They need to be given advance knowledge of the advantages of this new concept and a reason for buying it. So he hires a man to go out ahead of himself to prepare the people. The tradesman would then come with his new product, and the people would be ready to accept it."

"Please explain your parable," said the Chief Priest.

"The tradesman is the Messiah. The new product is a new expression of God's love for humanity. The hired man is Elijah, who will precede the Anointed One. It is my belief that is the meaning of the passage from Isaiah."

Philip noticed that John's body tensed as he was listening to Y'shua's comments.

The Chief Priest said, "Be more specific, please."

"The 'voice' is Elijah, the man who goes out ahead of the Messiah. 'The wilderness' is potential customers...the people of Judea who will have to change their way of thinking to accept the Messiah. The 'straight roadway' is the work of Elijah...the advance man...to prepare for the coming of the Anointed One." He sat down.

After a moment's silence, the Chief Priest said, "Thank you, Y'shua. ... That ... IS a new thinking on the passage." He paused, "Does anyone have any more comments or questions?"

After a moment of inaction, Aaron rose. He was acknowledged. "I request a meeting of the Council of the Many this afternoon."

"All right. We will gather here in two hours. Who do you want to interview?"

"John and Samuel."

"Do you want a private hearing or open for all?"

"Make it the option of the men," gesturing in the direction of John and Samuel.

Waving his hand, John said, "It matters not to me."

"Nor to me," added Samuel.

Looking around the room, the High Priest said, "It will be open, then, and we may interview others at the same meeting."

The intervening two hours were spent in rest and private. Philip went to the scriptorium to read some more of the Manual of Discipline. He was curious to learn about the Teacher of Righteousness. The man's name was never given. The manual was developed during his leadership. He was probably a priest, and knew the secrets of interpreting prophecy. The

"Wicked Priest," who wasn't identified, either, persecuted him.

Philip returned to the assembly hall to listen to the way the Council of Many operated. Also, he was curious why the Examiner had asked for a meeting to interview John and Samuel. Fifteen priests were seated on one side of the long table. Seated in the center was Aaron, the Examiner. Others that he recognized were Jesse, the man in charge of the kitchen, Joseph, his reader in the scriptorium, and Elihu, the watchman in the tower. Philip took a seat as far from the center as possible.

John and Samuel entered the room together and seated themselves across from Aaron. Other men from the community came in and scattered themselves around the room. The visitor, Y'shua, was among them.

When everyone was in place and settled, Aaron opened the meeting by addressing Samuel first, "Have you any questions on your heart?"

"No. I've been a part of this community for almost a year, and when I've had a question a member has been kind enough to provide me with the information."

"Have you any sin to confess?"

"Sir, I know that I have sinned...we cannot be human and be without sin. My sins are letting my mind stray from what I should have it on. I pray for forgiveness."

"You know our code of revealing our innermost thoughts. Are you willfully withholding anything from us?"

"No, sir."

Looking first right and left Aaron nodded and then said, "Are you in agreement with the Manual of Discipline?"

"Yes. It is my guide for daily living."

Turning to the other priests on the council Aaron asked, "Do any of you have any questions of Samuel?" The movements of heads indicated they did not.

"Samuel, the Council of the Many has decided to pass you from first-year probationer to second-year. This means, as you know, that you may bathe in the living water, and ..." reaching behind him to pick up a bundle, "...here is your ax, loin cloth and white robe. If all goes well after another year, you will be eligible to become a full member and eat with us."

Philip could tell that Samuel had not been prepared for advancement, and he seemed to be at a loss for words. As he took the bundle, he found his voice to say, "Thank you."

Now Aaron turned his attention to John. "Do you have any questions on your heart?"

"Yes, Mr. Examiner, I do."

When he seemed to hesitate, Aaron said, "Go ahead."

As if picking the right words John slowly said, "For the last six weeks to two months I've had an urgent call ... from God ... to leave this place and go out among the people ... and preach."

"How do you know your call is from God?"

Impatient with the question, John testily replied, "How did Elijah know the voice of God? I just know!"

"What are you being called to preach?"

Searching for the answer, John said, "I am to preach repentance of sins, and to baptize those who repent in the River Jordan. My feeling is that I am to prepare the way for the coming of the Messiah."

"We discerned this morning, when you gave a new meaning to the reading from Isaiah, that you had received an insight. We love you John, and do not want to stand in your way, but we also want you to be sure of your interpretation."

"The commission became more urgent when I heard the parable of the tradesman this morning."

Digesting this information, Aaron paused before saying, "You know, as a member of this covenant for more than ten years, if you leave here, you will be an outcast."

"Yes, I know."

"Because of the oath you have taken to eat no food not prepared by one of our priests, you will be committing yourself to a life of starvation."

"Yes, I realize the consequences of my leaving here," John replied testily, "but I also know that I must answer His call to go out and preach repentance of sins and baptize. My life and existence will be in His care."

"Then you have made your decision?"

The question hung there. Aaron looked at John, seeing a kind of wild strength in this intense man that he thought he knew. He realized that he had always felt John was a man with a glorious purpose in life and a role to fulfill in God's plan for His human creation.

Finally John said, "Yes. I'll go tomorrow morning. I'll leave my white robe here. Perhaps the tanner can provide me with a skin to wear?"

"All right. And the kitchen can give you a bag of food. We will miss you, but we wish you well."

"Thank you. The years here have been good training for me. If we do not see one another tomorrow morning, I shall say 'Shalom' to you now."

Philip felt he had been a witness to a tremendous event, although he couldn't identify the reason for the feeling.

## Chapter Seven

John had mixed emotions the next morning as he prayed with his brothers of the covenant for the last time. His future would be quite a contrast to the orderly life he had been living for the last twelve years. The unknown factor was challenging and very exciting. He was relieved the meeting had taken place the day before and pushed him into making a decision to go.

After prayer, he went to the tanner who greeted him, "Shalom, John. You are here for a skin to wear? I was at the meeting yesterday and heard you had received a call from God."

"Yes, I am leaving the covenant as an outcast. You heard Aaron give me permission for a hide. Do you have one?"

"I have been looking them over and have selected this one," picking up a large pelt. "I think it will be big enough for you, and should last you for a long time." It was sandy-beige colored, probably from a camel.

John removed his white robe, folding it carefully, and handed it to the tanner.

"Let us try this for size," as the skin was put around him. The tanner said, "I'll sew these two legs together to make an armhole, and lace this side to make it easy to get into. It won't take long." He removed it from John's shoulders.

A few minutes later John was given his garment, which he slipped into. It had a different feel than his cloth robe, which he expected. It was soft and more supple than he thought it would be.

The tanner handed him a leather belt and said, "This will help to keep it in place."

"Thank you very much. I appreciate all of this..."

"We will miss you, John. We feel God has chosen the right man to prepare the way for the coming Messiah. Shalom. God will be with you."

"Shalom, my friend. May God keep you well."

John left the tanner's and went to the kitchen. Jesse had prepared a large bag for him. "Here are some provisions that will help you for awhile," he said as he handed John the sack.

"I appreciate your caring, Jesse." He knew it would contain a variety of cheese, dried fruits and vegetables.

"Shalom, John. I wish I could go with you, but please know...in my heart, I am there. We will miss you."

John embraced Jesse and said, "Shalom, my friend. Thank you."

As John left the walled compound on the west side, Elihu, the tower watchman, who walked with him to the path down the ravine, joined him. "I always felt there was something special about you, John," he said as they walked along. "God be with you. Shalom." They embraced and parted.

*Here I am*, John thought as he started down the ravine: *Ties to the past have been cut. I have my loincloth, sandals, a skin garment, a bag of food, and faith in the Lord. And I am almost happy! I feel like a child starting on a big adventure.*

John's youth had provided him with few adventures. His parents, Zechariah and Elizabeth, were very old when he, an only child, was born. His father was the village priest, so it was assumed that John would be the successor when his father died. His early upbringing was with that in mind. John was fourteen when his father died—too young to assume the important post in the opinion of the High Priest in Jerusalem. So someone else was sent to fill the position. Soon thereafter his mother died. John's care and upbringing was put in the hands of his sect, "the Holy Ones." Then twelve years ago, when he was eighteen, he came to Qumran, accepted the vows of the covenant, and expected to live there the rest of his life. His reason for coming, he reflected, was for the cause he believed in—purity of the scriptures, and protest against the imposter priests in Jerusalem. And, too, he did not know what else to do with his life. Up to that time it had been a disappointment.

John was thinking over these things as he walked down the trail toward Jericho. His mother had told him a story about how an angel had appeared to his father on one of his weeks of duty in the Temple in Jerusalem. The angel had told his father that Elizabeth was going to have a baby boy, and he was to be given the name of John. Elizabeth was old, beyond the time of childbearing, but the angel insisted. For doubting, his father lost his voice until John was born. His mother told him, "You are special. God brought you into the world for a specific purpose."

He hadn't thought of that story for a long time. Because of his expectation of succeeding his father, and his mother's belief that he was special, he remembered how angry he became over being denied his birthright. He suddenly realized he still felt that way to this very day. In looking back he realized that he would have had a hard time gaining the villagers respect had he been a fourteen-year-old priest. Nevertheless, he was convinced that the priesthood in Jerusalem was corrupt and they and the rest of the people of the nation needed to repent of their sins. He also realized his upbringing of being somebody special had influenced his self-esteem. It had never left him even if he did not think of his mother's story very often. It was always in the corner of his mind.

His thoughts turned to the visitor Y'shua. He was one of John's many cousins. The Sons of Zadok were all descended from a common ancestor, so all of the priests at Qumran were related to each other. But Y'shua's relationship to him was on their mothers' side. Before John's mother died, Y'shua's mother came and visited periodically. He remembered playing with Y'shua when they were both very young. John was older than he by six months, and—to get his way—he would remind Y'shua of that fact. He had not seen Y'shua for many years. His heart had leapt when he saw him, just as it did when he was a child. *What is there about that person to cause me to react the way I do? What had brought Y'shua to Qumran?*

The smell of salt water told John he was nearing the lake below Qumran. The thought of bathing in the flowing Jordan was stimulating. The greenery along the river was visible ahead of him. He left the path to go into the bushes and trees. Putting down the food sack, taking off his hairy garment, loincloth, and sandals, he waded into the river. After the long, hot, dusty walk down the ravine, this cool, flowing water was a welcome relief. Following the bath, he prayed and ate a light meal from the rations with which Jesse provided him. Taking stock, he thought: *I must make this last as long as possible. I know God will help me find enough food from the wild to sustain life when it is gone, but I must be frugal.*

He dressed, went back to the path heading north toward the intersection to Jericho. It was an important crossroad. Jerusalem was beyond Jericho to the southwest, and Bethel and the beautiful Jezreel Valley to the north on this, the west side of the river. Across the river was the main road to the Sea of Galilee and points north and to the east. He knew he must go where the people were to preach his call for repentance, but the flowing stream was calling him. Turning away from Jericho, he headed toward the Jordan.

The sun was past the halfway point. John decided to look for a shady spot in which to wait for the heat of the afternoon to subside. He could see such a place on the other side where other travelers were resting. John waded into the water, forded the river, which was shallow at that location. He put his bag down near a friendly-looking man.

"Shalom," the man said as John seated himself on the ground.

"Shalom," John replied. "What brings you to the river today?"

John learned that he was a courier for a merchant. He had a wagonload of goods consigned to Herod Antipas' fortress at Machaerus, east of the Dead Sea, also known as Lake Asphaltitus or Salt Sea.

John said, "I've been in the wilderness for twelve years. What has been happening in the world?"

"Twelve years? In the wilderness?" His eyes seemed to protrude as he stared at John's face, then took in his camel skin garment.

"That's a long time!" Scratching his head and looking off into space, he said, "Where shall I start? The country is filled with unrest. Ah, yes!" His face brightened. "A new Roman governor has come. His name is Pontius Pilate. The people of Judea do not know yet what he is like."

"Is Annas still High Priest?"

"No," he said as he waved his arm in disgust, "he was deposed years ago. But his son-in-law, Joseph Caiaphas, was appointed, so Annas still has much influence."

John, fingering his beard in thought commented, "The temple is still playing politics, I see."

"Say! You probably don't know about Antipas' taking Herod's wife, Herodias, do you?"

"No. Now let me think...Herod was one of Old Herod's sons." John thought *I really have been in the wilderness too long...I am having trouble remembering the genealogy of our country's rulers.*

His friend said, "Yes."

"Wasn't his mother...Mariamne, daughter of Simon the High Priest?"

"Yes, that is right. And Herodias is the granddaughter of Old Herod through his Hasmonean wife, also named Mariamne."

John, sensing something more important than what he was hearing said, "Well…what happened to Herod, the younger?"

"Oh," shaking his head, "He was disinherited a long time ago."

"Ah! Yes. Now I remember. Old Herod's will named three of his sons as tetrarchs over different parts of his kingdom. Archelaus was supposed to be king of what is now Judea, but he was the one banished by Rome."

"You are right…he surely was," said the courier, studying John's face.

"Well," John said thoughtfully, "If Herodias has married Antipas, surely her husband has died?"

"No! He has not died!" the courier exclaimed.

John, who had been lying back, sat upright. The courier also sat up and continued, "And neither has Antipas' wife…he divorced her. Her father is stirring up trouble with him, too."

"What?" cried John. "I cannot believe what I am hearing!"

"Herodias and her daughter, Salome, are now with Antipas in his kingdom of Galilee and Perea. They may be at Machaerus now."

"Why…why that is…how dare he? Adultery! That makes her an adulteress!" John almost shouted. Other resting travelers looked his way.

"Yes," his acquaintance answered, "Adultery, selfishness and greed are rampant throughout the nation. Some people are saying the only way the world can be saved is by the Messiah coming and taking charge of all the governments."

Half rising and in a loud voice, incensed with anger, John said, "Repentance must come first!"

The man he had been visiting with also arose to a more alert position, as did all the travelers who had been resting.

John became aware that he had their attention. He thought: *so this is it...this is what I have been called to do. I have no need to go to the cities. I can stay right here and reach the people.* So he stood upright. He studied the people, wondering how best to start. He cleared his throat and tried to calm his disgust and contempt of the situation he had just come to know. He found words in his mouth, ready and waiting to be said.

"I have just learned of the sinful example the ruler of this country has set. Does he not know that his position requires him to be bound by the Laws of Moses?" His voice became more strident and agitated. He realized he must control himself. The travelers rearranged themselves so they could face this unusual speaker garbed in camel skin.

"Does he not know that this adulterous situation is an insult to the followers of Father Abraham? The time is at hand when all people need to examine their own way of life. Does it measure up to the Laws of Moses?" In a loud and strong voice, he shouted, "Repent of your sins. This is absolutely necessary, especially now that our ruler is setting such a sinful example!"

Someone spoke up. "First, sir, tell us who you are."

Standing erect, presenting a powerful image of strength, he answered, "I am John, the voice crying in the wilderness."

"What does it mean to repent?" someone called from the edge of the shaded area.

"Repentance is saying you have done something wrong and you are truly sorry. You have cheated or lied, robbed or killed. You have dishonored your parents, your wife or children. Do you still love God with all your heart, soul and mind? Do you tell your children of His great love every chance you get?" A rustle came from the crowd as people looked at one another, chuckling as they recognized themselves in John's description.

"Confessing your wrongdoings is part of repentance. You need to go beyond that and ask forgiveness from the person you wronged, as well as from God."

"What happens to us if we repent?"

John shifted his posture. "What happens? You will experience a feeling of intense love. Clearing your mind of all your guilt that only you and God knows deep within yourselves, you can be free of all your old ways, and start a new sin-free life."

As eyes from the audience fastened on him, John realized he was giving these people a hope they never had. He became more confident that he was doing the right thing. He interacted with the people, and his emotions began to be heard in the words tumbling out of his mouth.

"You will want to tell the world of God's magnificence." Then he added, "If you commit yourself to a life worthy of the kingdom of God, I shall baptize you right here and now in the Jordan."

"We do not understand the word 'baptize.' Is it a tradition that we do not know about? Explain it to us, John."

John thought: I have been out of touch with the people too long. They have received very little training.

"I can tell that tradition is important to you…as it is to me. When our people were in captivity in Babylon, some went over to the Babylonian ways, but many remained true to God's Laws. Their dedication and purity attracted some Gentiles to come over to our religion. Baptism, that is immersing the whole body under water, was used as a symbol of cleansing the newcomer of all his old habits and beliefs. It was used as a rite that an initiate had to undergo. It was not repeated. Also, Jews who returned to worshiping God were baptized. So, it is an accepted tradition that has not been used since our people returned to our homeland. I am reviving baptism now as a symbol for anyone to be ready to enter the kingdom of God, for we have all sinned and fallen away from the Law."

As John paused momentarily, he heard, "Preach to us some more, John." "Tell us more," as though they were hungry for this kind of straight talk. So he preached until first one and then another came to him to repent of their sins. As he took off his outer clothes, he asked them to do the same. They waded into the river and he baptized them.

John's message was carried wherever travelers went. People started coming to the river just to hear him preach.  Some followers became disciples and listened to him every chance they had.

During the hours before and after his preaching and baptizing John visited with the people.  To those who needed it he gave advice and counsel.  He told them, "If you have two coats, share one with someone who has none.  If people have no food, share what you have with them."

Tax collectors came to repent and be baptized.  To them he said, "Do not collect any more taxes from the people than what they owe."  And to soldiers, "Be content with your wages, and do not use your power as a soldier to cause people to fear you."

Some individuals experienced a healing after repenting their sins and receiving the baptism.  The first time it happened John was as surprised as the one who was made well.  They both praised the Lord.

The more John visited, counseled, and cared for the people, the more he felt that at last he was a real priest.  His congregation just happened to be travelers passing through the Jordan and his synagogue was the great outdoors.

The ruling priests in Jerusalem came out to ask him if he were the Messiah, to which he answered, "No!  I am not!  There is someone coming after me whose sandals I am not worthy to untie."

The crowds he was attracting were a worry to the Pharisees and Scribes from Jerusalem.  Also, John's judgment of Antipas reached his ears, and Herodias took a disliking to John.

# Chapter Eight

After the food in his bag was gone, John ate wild honey, berries and grasshoppers. He threaded a twig through their bodies and roasted them over the coals of a bonfire.

People offered to share their food, but he always declined. When friends from Qumran came down to bathe in the river, they brought food for him. These gifts he accepted.

He found a small cave near the river where he slept during the cooler nights. He seemed to thrive under his chosen circumstances.

One morning, after about six months of preaching, John awakened with the excited feeling that somehow this was to be an extraordinary day. However, the sky did not reflect his buoyant feeling—it was partially overcast. Although it was early spring, nearing the time of Passover, the air was unusually warm, and heavy with moisture. Thunder was heard in the distance.

As he went among the crowd before he started preaching, he found himself looking for someone special—who exactly, he didn't know. A great many people stayed at the Jordan with him for days at a time. Travelers would come and go, about the same number as before he started his ministry. He had become acquainted with many of his followers.

He looked out over the crowd as he preached, still looking for that special someone. The day went as most except when he was in the Jordan baptizing.

From out of nowhere came a quickening of flesh from his scalp to his toes. At first he thought he had been struck by lightning. Then he saw the man next in line was his cousin Y'shua! His heart leapt. He had not seen him in the crowd—where did he come from?

Suddenly he felt a need for Y'shua's approval—no longer was he the more privileged elder cousin. He said, "You should be baptizing me, not I you."

Y'shua replied, "We need to do everything right. And it is right that you baptize me this day."

John was awed by his feeling of unworthiness and was intimidated to be so bold as to put his hand on Y'shua's flesh. (Robes were left on the riverbank.) Y'shua's bright blue eyes bored into John's. Finally, John took hold of his body and immersed it in the flowing waters of the Jordan.

Immediately upon coming out of the water, a ray of sun from the partly cloudy sky fell on Y'shua. For just a moment a brilliant light shone above his head! No, it was a bird—a dove—briefly over Y'shua's shoulder and quickly flying away!

A sudden clap of thunder sounded like the voice of God approving this action. To John's mind came the words, *"This is my beloved son, with whom I am pleased."*

*What am I hearing? Is Y'shua the Messiah? Had he too heard the voice of God?* John looked into the eyes of his cousin, standing dripping before him. They seemed like two enormous pools of power. Water trickled down from his hair over a face he'd never before considered beautiful, but was today.

Y'shua moved on.   John watched as he walked back to shore.   He thought: *could he actually be the one we have been waiting for?   Is he the reason for my being here today?*

John felt charged with new life.   *I think I have seen the Anointed One!*   He wondered: *how can I be sure?   I will know some day*, he answered himself.

The few men remaining in the water to be baptized received the benefit of his new energy.   Later he learned they had also experienced a similar tingling of flesh.

## Chapter Nine

The women in camp at Qumran continued to pique Philip's interest. He would look for them at prayer time, trying to determine—from a distance—what their ages might be. Before going to sleep he found himself in a fantasy, meeting one accidentally and becoming acquainted with her. Then they met secretly in a secluded location and he shared himself with her. She was always beautiful, a little younger than he, and very sympathetic.

Then one evening, when he was outside taking a walk around the compound, he nearly bumped into one of the women. "I'm sorry," he said.

She answered, "I didn't see you. It's my fault." She wasn't as beautiful as the girl in his fantasy, but she was about twenty-five years old. She hurried past him and went on her way. This chance meeting excited him, and gave form to his daydreams. However, he never saw her again, even though he looked for her.

He knew his thoughts were sinful. Try as he would to battle his imagination just before sleep, it seemed to have full reign of his mental faculty. He couldn't free himself of it. The next night, and the next would be the same. The guilt of these, along with his continued night dreams of Hannah, worked together to cause more stress. He reached the point where he didn't know what was worse: letting his dream world absorb him, or fighting this stressful feeling of guilt. It was beginning to take its toll, robbing him of energy and strength in his legs.

Philip's days at Qumran became a blur of sameness for six days a week. The Sabbath Day broke the monotony. He looked forward to the exchange of ideas that expanded the meaning of the scriptures. He learned more of the governing of the place from the Manual of Discipline and was in agreement with most of it. However, he was beginning to feel the factor of exclusivity was wrong, and the ritualistic bathing was made too important, as well as being discriminatory. He kept these feelings to himself, and with them came more stiffness. He had started using a walking stick to help keep his balance, and found that it gave him a degree of stability and confidence of movement.

One morning in the scriptorium, as Philip struggled to rise to his feet after sitting for several hours, he was unable to make his legs support the weight of his body. He grabbed at the writing table, twisting his wrist, as he was going down, but couldn't break the fall. The next thing he knew he was on the floor. "What is happening to me?" he asked aloud.

The scriptorium was filled with priest-readers and scriveners, now that the harvest had been completed and their help no longer needed in the fields and gardens. Those near Philip came running to assist him. Joseph asked, "Philip! Are you hurt?"

"No. Nothing serious, anyway," he answered as he attempted to maneuver his legs under him. He reached for the writing table for leverage to try again to stand.

His wrist hurt and his face smarted from abrasions. His hands started to shake.

"Here, let me help you." Joseph and one of the others reached down to give him support under his arms.

"Thank you," Philip said as he sat again on his bench. "I don't know why I am losing strength in my legs. I just do not understand it. I have always been so healthy and strong."

"Do you think you could get around if you had crutches?"

Crutches! The very thought was loathsome. To Philip they were a symbol of hopelessness and helplessness. Then he thought: *pride and vanity. I have no room for either with my legs turning to liquid. Here I am, having to be helped up off the floor.*

"Yes, I think they may help. I do appreciate the offer."

"Good. We will get some for you. People have come here and been healed. When they went away, they left them here. I think we can find a pair that will be right for you."

So Philip was fitted with a pair of crutches. It took a month for him to get used to them—sore spots under his arms and the muscles in his shoulders and arms hurt—but they provided him with some independence. He was grateful for that. Once on his feet and balanced, he could make his legs do some of the work. They were not completely paralyzed.

"You said that people came here crippled and received a healing. What did they do?" he asked Joseph one day.

57

"The High Priest has a special service. It has been quite some time since we have had one. I'll talk to him about it. He interviews all those who wish to participate. If you want, I'll tell him that you are interested. He will call you to talk to him."

"Thank you, Joseph. I'd be most grateful, if you would."

Philip had not spoken with the High Priest since he came to Qumran. He was impressed with the fairness of his actions and behavior during the Sabbath discussions of scripture. Philip was anxious to have the interview, to find out what it was all about, and to attend the healing service. So, when the call came, Philip was ready. The meeting was to be in the assembly hall.

"Shalom, Philip. Come in and sit across from me.

"Shalom." Philip seated himself.

"Joseph tells me that you are becoming disabled and would like to attend a healing service."

"Yes, sir. I would very much."

"Tell me about yourself and this impairment."

"I came here about six months ago. I walked from Bethsaida, my home village. It took me four days. I had no difficulty and felt in good health. Since I've been here, I have been Joseph's scribe in the scriptorium. This condition began as a feeling of stiffness. I thought it was from inactivity. And it has worsened to where I need these crutches to help me walk."

"What kind of exercises have you tried?"

"I have not done any recently. At first I would try to walk around the compound before going to bed. But it has progressed to the point that now I must use these crutches."

"Have you sinned?"

Philip was not ready for such a blunt question. He hesitated, glancing down before answering, and slowly replied, "I am not quite sure…and it embarrasses me."

"You are not quite sure?" he echoed with raised eyebrows.

"No sir, I am not." Taking a deep breath he continued, "This seems to happen as I am falling to sleep, and I have no control." He paused.

"Go, ahead. Your secrets are safe with me."

"Well, sir," Philip looked the High Priest in the eye and said sheepishly, "I am having a fantasy relationship with one of the women here at the compound."

The High Priest frowned slightly. "It is just a fantasy?"

"Oh, yes, sir! One evening I nearly ran into one, but she went her way and I went mine…. But my thoughts return to her in that half-dream state just as I go to sleep, almost every night."

"Are you married?"

"I have been. My wife died in childbirth about three months before I came here."

"Do you miss being with a woman?"

"Yes, sir, I do. I loved my wife and I still grieve her loss. I feel that I am being disloyal to her by participating in this fantasy, even though I can not control it."

"Well, you have done the right thing in confessing it to me. You know the Commandment. We teach here that to even look at a woman with lust or think about it is an act of adultery. Is there anything else you need to confess?"

"No, I don't think so." His guilt regarding Hannah's death had become so much a part of him that it didn't occur to Philip to disclose that secret, nor his disagreement with some of the Rules of Discipline.

"You are a good candidate for healing. I'll pray for your forgiveness. We believe God has a natural remedy for every ailment. I shall study the manuscripts for the plant that is good for paralysis."

Philip nodded approval.

The priest continued, "When you go for meals, Jesse will see that you are served the tea." He reached into a box and brought out a smooth pebble about the size of a plum. "We also use healing stones. God has blessed certain kinds of rocks. Sometimes they help." Handing it to Philip, he said, "Take this and carry it with you. Rub it when you think of it."

He stood as though the interview was over. Philip said, "Thank you, sir. I'll let you know of my progress."

"Yes, do that. If these don't work, we will include you in a healing service. We'll be planning one before long."

Philip drank the tea and rubbed the stone. He did become stronger at first and then no more improvement. Jacob told him about a month later that the High Priest was preparing a healing service the morning after the Sabbath, and Philip was invited to attend.

"Can you tell me about it?"

"We begin with a bath in the living water. By that I mean the flowing water. Afterward we have a sacred meal and then he prays for each candidate."

"I am looking forward to it."

The day after the Sabbath was three days away. Philip could hardly wait. At last the day came. After Morning Prayer, those who made the trip to Qumran for healing assembled in the bathing room. Priests assisted them to disrobe and enter the pool. A very gentle small stream was flowing from a conduit into the pool and out the other side. Steps led the bathers into the water. Those that couldn't manage the steps sat on the edge with their legs dangling into the bath. The cool water was stimulating to Philip, and he was able to go into the deep part.

When all were in the water, or seated on the edge, the High Priest said, "The bath we are participating in today is a washing for purification, physical or spiritual or both." And then he prayed, "O God, hear our prayer. Your servants have confessed their sins, and petition for healing to their bodies and souls. Now as we symbolically wash away the putridness, may Your healing be made manifest. Amen."

After the bath and dressing, the candidates and priests went into the assembly room. As Philip traversed the distance on his crutches he wondered *are my legs really stronger, or am I just wishing?*

Places had been set for a meal. Wine was on the table. The High Priest occupied the position at the center of the dais. The other priests stood at the sides. Candidates were seated at the table. The High Priest gave a short sermon on the cause of illness:

transgressions of God's laws. Healing comes when God forgives the transgression.

A platter of roasted lamb and vegetables was brought in and placed on the altar behind the High Priest. He said, "This is a sacred meal. God is unhappy with animal sacrifices on the altar. We select the most pure animal for our sacred meals. It is slaughtered according to the Laws of Moses. Our people prepare it." He said this to inform the visitors who may not have known the strictness observed at Qumran regarding food and eating.

"Priests have eaten sacrificial meat from the beginning of the priesthood. We are priests, so we will eat. Let us pray: O God, hear our prayer. Thank You for providing a perfect animal as a symbol of your perfection. We have gathered here to partake of Your will for our bodies and souls. We pray Your blessings on this food. May healing take place this day. Amen.

"Each will come forward to be anointed with oil and receive your sacred meal."

The priests assisted those who needed it to go to the dais. Philip was able to maneuver by himself. The High Priest dipped his hand in a bowl of olive oil and placed it on the head of each man saying, "Blessed be the God of Abraham, Isaac and Jacob. You are anointed as a son of Abraham. Go with God." A plate with a small piece of the roasted meat and a portion of the vegetables was given to each man. They took it back to their place at the table and ate. The priests served themselves last, and also sat at the table to eat.

After the meal, the candidates went to the dais and knelt. The High Priest prayed again for their healing, and several among candidates said, "Yes, I am well," or, "I am free of the pain!" Philip knew his legs were stronger, but he didn't feel like giving up his crutches. He was disappointed, but consoled himself with the thought that maybe it will take some time. After the service, he and Joseph, who had been assisting, went to the scriptorium to work on the manuscripts.

## Chapter Ten

Days passed, and Philip's legs didn't get any better. For a week they seemed to be stronger than they were before the healing service, but then they returned to their former weakness. He continued to have his dream-state rendezvous with the unknown woman, and he believed that to be the cause of his relapse.

Then came the morning when his legs were limp and he couldn't walk up the path from the cave for Morning Prayer. He couldn't even crawl! He was paralyzed! When he didn't appear in the scriptorium, Joseph came to the cave to see if he were still there.

"Philip, are you in there?" he called into the cave.

"Yes, Joseph. I need some help to get up the path...I can't make it."

Joseph entered the cave. "If you lean on me, do you think you can walk?"

"My knees won't support me...I can't even crawl."

"Are you in pain?"

"Only the pain of embarrassment that this is happening to me. I feel no physical pain."

"I'll get some help to carry your litter to the scriptorium."

Joseph left the cave to return a little later with the tanner and two men from the kitchen. They brought with them two poles. The tanner laced Philip's goatskin securely to the poles in litter fashion. Philip was lifted on to the litter. Each man then took an end and lifted Philip on his bed and carried him up the path and into the scriptorium. There they put the litter down and lifted Philip to the bench at his writing table. He was able to sit and write.

Philip had a hard time concentrating on what Joseph was reading to him. His thoughts kept returning to what was happening to his body. *How could he continue living here in this condition? What had brought it on? How could he manage to get to the kitchen? What about his personal toiletry?*

When the meal break came, the two helpers from the kitchen came with a small wagon they used to transport produce. They lifted Philip into it and pulled it to the kitchen, where they helped him with his personal needs. Then he was seated at the table.

A new visitor was at the table with them that day. The senior member introduced him as Zoheth, a disciple of John. Conversation during the meal was encouraged, as everyone was anxious to learn about John and how he was getting along as an outcast.

Zoheth reported that he was preaching reform and preparation for the coming of the Messiah. He was summoning people into the "wilderness" to meet God, away from their creature comforts. And they were coming. Zoheth said, "He called some Pharisees and Sadducees a brood of serpents, when they came for baptism. He told them not to presume to be secure with God, just because they were sons of Abraham."

Someone said, "That sounds like John. He speaks his mind. Tell us more about his baptisms."

"He preaches one baptism as a washing away of all sins. It symbolizes moral renewal and an initiation into a life of purity. He has been surprised that some people have received physical healing after having confessed their sins and being baptized."

*Healing!* Philip's mind couldn't stay with the remainder of Zoheth's report. His thoughts started searching for a way to get down to the river.

Philip was carried to his cave and his pallet was put in its usual place, but sleep didn't come.

"Samuel?" The whisper broke the silence like a clap of thunder, "Are you still awake?"

"If I weren't, I am now. What is it, Philip?"

"I've been thinking that if I can get to John down on the Jordan and be baptized by him, I know I will be healed! The men in this cave are my friends, aren't they? Will they help to carry me down?"

"Philip," a whispered reply from the dark cave answered, "Do you realize that you will be cast out of the brotherhood, like John was, just for thinking about going? Furthermore, we could be cast out for helping you."

"Yes, I know the risk I'll be taking, but the leaders won't punish you for helping me. I'm sure," Philip answered.

Another whisper from the darkness asked, "Didn't you go to the High Priest for a healing? What happened?"

"Except for a brief feeling of being stronger in my legs, nothing has changed."

From another direction, "It seems peculiar the way your paralysis came on you. Do you have any explanation? Did you fall or have a fever?"

Philip spoke aloud, now being aware of everyone being awake, "No, I haven't fallen, except after this started to come on, nor did I have a fever. And I don't know why I have gradually become paralyzed from the waist down. I feel no pain, only frustration. Oh, I'm a little aggravated with some of the rules here."

"I thought you were in agreement with the philosophy of the Teacher of Righteousness. What bothers you?"

"I agree with preserving the purity of the scriptures we are doing, the communal sharing, the hospitality we show to visitors, and most of the philosophies of the Teacher of Righteousness. What disturbs me is our exclusiveness, and the ritual baths. I believe in cleanliness, but three times a day! And just for full members, too, that bothers me. John preaches one immersion cleanses for a lifetime. And he invites anyone to submit his will to the Lord God." He paused a moment and said, "I want to go to John."

"How do you know so much about John?"

"We had a visitor who is a follower of John's. People are calling him the Baptist, because of his immersing believers in the Jordan."

"What else is John saying or doing?"

"He is preaching repentance of sins, and sharing. He says, 'He who has two coats, let him share one with him who has none,' and the same with food. Just like we do here. He also is saying that someone is coming after him who will be greater than he...that he, John, is not the Messiah."

Silence fell on the whispering group and then one said, "Let's think on how we can help you. Now try to get some sleep."

The next day Aaron, the Examiner, sent Jesse to summon Philip for an interview after the second meal. Philip said, "I wonder what this is about." Jesse answered, "It may have to do with your wish to see John."

Philip stared at Jesse. *How could he know?*

The men from the kitchen carried Philip on his litter to the assembly room and helped him to sit on a seat across from Aaron.

"Shalom, Philip," said Aaron.

"Shalom, Aaron."

"I am told that you would like to go to John down on the Jordan to have him heal you."

Looking Aaron in the eye, Philip said, "Yes, sir, I would. His follower said miracles have happened after his baptisms. My paralytic condition is getting worse, and I'm ready for a miracle. May I have your permission to go?"

"First I need to know what you will do if you are not healed?"

Philip sensed a hope that he would be given a chance to go. He realized his future would be determined by his answer so he must speak truthfully.

"I...am a burden on the men here. It requires two men to carry me around. That takes them away from their assigned work. So ...if I'm not healed, I'll return to my home village at Bethsaida, if I can get there."

"And if you are healed?"

"Well, sir...if I am healed and can walk again, I'll return to the compound, if it meets your approval."

"You are a good man, Philip. Joseph is well pleased with your work in the scriptorium. I shall do what I can to help you."

Philip found himself smiling and Aaron continued, "This time of year we can spare the men. Tomorrow, after our morning meal, we will see that you get down to the river where John is preaching. You will come back here in either event—to stay if you are healed or to prepare for the trip to your village if you are not."

"Thank you, sir. It means so much to me. Thank you."

The men were summoned to carry Philip to his cave.

Philip's morning prayer was more intense than it had been in a long time. He was full of praise and adoration, plus prayers for John, Aaron, the High Priest, and the men who were going to carry him down the hill. In the scriptorium he had a sense of foreboding that he couldn't quite identify. *Am I happy, or not? Why this feeling of anxiety? Was there to be an accident on the way to the river?*

Time for the morning meal finally came. Philip was helped to the kitchen where he washed and ate. He felt that he was rushing his food, impatient to be on the way to the river. When he and the men who had been carrying him had finished, they put him on his litter and carried him out the kitchen door. A donkey, hitched to a produce wagon, was waiting there. The men loaded him into the wagon. Off they went in the direction of the gardens and fields. The men walked alongside the donkey.

"I haven't been this way before," Philip said.

"The distance may be farther this way, but the grade is more gentle and easier on the animal."

Philip was grateful for the opportunity to see the fields, orchards, vineyards and gardens, even though it was the off-season and only a few crops were growing. The gardens were about two miles from the compound in a dry watercourse, protected by cliffs on each side of the delta. Fresh water springs made the location an oasis in the desert. Irrigation channels from the springs led to all parts of the acreage. A variety of trees gave the compound an abundance of fruit, and a vineyard provided grapes for the wine. Now Philip knew why most of the men at the compound worked in the gardens during the growing season—care of all this required much labor.

The road to Jericho was not far from the lower end of the gardens. When the wagon party reached the road they followed it until it was intersected by the Jericho road from across the river. They turned toward the river. As they neared the water, they could hear John's voice preaching. Philip felt that this is too good to be true*: yesterday I was hoping to come here, and today—here I am, hearing John for myself!*

The little donkey stopped as he entered the water, put his mouth in the water and took a refreshing drink. The serenity of the place impressed Philip: The flowing water, blue sky, trees along the banks providing shade, people taking their ease on the ground across the river, listening to John who was standing on a slight rise near the water.

Philip had a hard time reconciling this wild man wearing a camel skin with the John he had met in Qumran robed in white. Now his words became

70

intelligible and he recognized his voice: "The seventh commandment God gave to Moses was 'You shall not commit adultery.' This means not only is it a sin to actually lie with a woman out of wedlock, but to look at one with eyes of lust is adultery! God wants the offspring of His chosen people to be conceived in the sanctity of marriage.

"Look at old King Herod's son, Antipas, who rules this territory. He has transgressed God's Law. He has taken his living brother's wife as his own. Both Antipas and Herodias are adulterers!"

The little wagon party had not yet moved into the water.

Suddenly, from the crowd of people on the other side, four of Antipas' soldiers stood, as if on cue, rushed to John and shouted, "You're under arrest!"

"What for? Preaching the truth?" John asked loudly.

"Inciting the people." They started to tie his wrists. John stepped backward, falling into the water. They followed him, splashing, into the river.

The people, not expecting this turn of events, suddenly came to their feet. A few reached the soldiers to defend John.

"Stand back!" commanded one of the soldiers.

John was now on his feet yelling, "Do you serve God or Antipas?"

Surprised, the soldier hesitated before answering, "We would be flogged if we didn't bring you in. We must do as he says," as he grabbed John's wrists.

More of the crowd came against the arresting party. One of the soldiers had a whip and cracked it at the attackers.

The people hung back.

After John's hands were tied together in front of him, they pulled him to the riverbank and his ankles were fettered with irons and chain. A rope was put around his neck, and he was hauled to where the horses were. The soldiers mounted their horses and led him away. The people were stunned into silence by this sudden loss of their leader. A few picked up their belongings and followed after him.

Philip couldn't believe what he had just witnessed. John arrested and taken away! *Why did this happen to John? Why? He was a man of God, preaching repentance. He hadn't actually hurt Antipas and Herodias. Who would have thought that what a preacher—a wild-looking man who wore a camel skin coat and lived in the desert—had to say about the ruler would be important enough to get him arrested?* All at once he wanted to lie down in the little wagon and never get up. His one hope of being healed had disappeared. What kind of a future did he have with this paralyzed body? Philip wept.

## Chapter Eleven

*Will this jostling never cease?* Philip questioned himself on the ride back to Qumran. No conversation took place. It was a dreary trip. Now he knew there was no choice but that he must try to go home to Bethsaida.

A welcome break came when the party rested at one of the yet running garden springs. They bathed and ate food that had been brought along, as they knew it would be past the evening meal when they returned.

"Did you find John?" called Elihu, the watchman, heralding their arrival as they crested the rise.

One of the men answered, "Yes, we found him, just in time to see him get arrested!"

"Arrested! … What for?"

The scene was described for Elihu as they walked by the wagon toward the compound. He said, "I must go to Aaron and tell him." And off he went on the run.

By the time the wagon party reached the kitchen door Aaron was there waiting. A frown told of his concern. "Philip, I'm so sorry."

"Thank you, Aaron. It seems that God doesn't want me to get healed."

"Are you still of a mind to return to your village?"

"Yes. If I can get a message to my brothers, I know they would come after me."

"Well, we will help you to your cave tonight and talk some more tomorrow."

73

So ended one long, disappointing day.

The interview with Aaron was scheduled to take place after the morning meal, inasmuch as Sabbath began at sundown the next day.

Philip was carried in and lifted to a seat opposite Aaron, who sat with his hands together on the table.

"Shalom, Philip."

"Shalom, Aaron. I am sorry to be so much trouble for you and the men who carry me around."

"We love you, Philip." He separated his hands in a palms-up gesture; placing them together again, continued, "We're sorry that this paralysis has come over you, and you have not been healed." Opening one hand asked, "Are you sure that you want to return to your village?"

With no hesitation Philip answered, "Yes! I think it would be for the best."

Aaron realized Philip had given it thought when Philip asked, "Do you have anyone making a delivery that could take a message to my family in Bethsaida?"

Shaking his head and glancing away, Aaron answered, "No, ...not soon." His countenance brightening, he asked, "How uncomfortable was it for you to travel in the produce wagon?"

Philip hesitated, reflecting on the experiences of the day before, slowly replied, "Well...it wasn't too bad on the way down, when my expectations were high. But I became very tired on the return trip."

Aaron eagerly asked, "If you had a bed of hay, do you think you could tolerate the discomfort of it for the four or five days it would take?"

Philip studied Aaron's face for a moment before asking, "You mean you would allow your men to take me home?" He hadn't expected this offer.

Aaron's folded hands were under his chin as he answered, "If that would be all right with you. The men can be spared this time of year, and it will provide them a chance to see the world they have put behind."

Philip fought to control the feeling welling up within. He thought: *these dear friends wanting, without hesitation, to go the extra mile or two, or three, because of their love and genuine concern for me.*

He was cautious when he finally spoke—he didn't want his voice to break. "It is generous of you...and I am grateful...to accept your offer."

Aaron was smiling. Philip's spirit lifted...he would be starting home much sooner than he expected. "It took me four days to walk it. With an animal, it may take a little longer." As though he was thinking aloud, he continued, "We'll rest tomorrow, of course, it being the Sabbath, but if we were to get our food provisions together the day after and leave the following day, we'll be sure to be in my village for the next Sabbath."

"Good! That will give the men and animal a little rest before they return." Aaron smiled as he continued, "So, we will plan it that way."

"Thank you, Aaron." Philip swallowed, tears beginning to well in his eyes. "Everyone here has been very kind to me. I love everyone that I have met, and I'll miss all of them. And you, Brother Aaron, you have been the most caring person I have known. It saddens me to have to leave this way."

"We want the best for you, Philip." He hesitated before continuing, holding one hand toward Philip, "I am impressed to prophesy that you will receive a healing someday." He paused, then said, "And when you do, you will have a...very special role to play in fulfilling God's plan for your life."

The first smile in a long while appeared on Philip's face. "That gives me ...oh" .... His voice broke, then continued in a slightly higher pitch, "...so much hope." Unable to voice his thoughts, he whispered, "Thank you."

As though Aaron wanted to control his own emotions, he hurriedly said, "All right, then. The wagon will be ready to depart right after Morning Prayer, two days after tomorrow. Our love goes with you."

and Mary, Philip's parents,
hat did not include Philip.
over by other members of
and by none more than his
, Phoebe, the elder, and
had grown accustomed to
th as a substitute mother,
d. Elizabeth was teaching
actical side of religion—the
, and what to eat on special
arn how to clean and comb
n into strands to be woven

se to Elizabeth to have the
wn the stairs early one
n she had seen them since
bright with smiles.
ng home!" Phoebe almost

k your daddy is coming

nd so did I. We had the
me in a wagon pulled by a

are of the twins reported
e was skeptical. "Why

would your father come home, and especially in a wagon?"

Prisca answered, "He couldn't walk...

Phoebe finished, "He had to be carried."

Concern showed on Elizabeth's face. *Should she take these children's fantasy seriously?* "Why couldn't he walk?"

"His legs..." Prisca couldn't find a word to express Philip's condition.

"What about his legs?" Elizabeth found herself becoming involved in the children's dream.

Phoebe said, "He couldn't use them."

"Were they broken?"

The twins solemnly looked at each other. Phoebe finally almost whispered, "We don't know."

The joy they had expressed at the foreknowledge of their father's return had faded. Now they realized that he was coming home a sick man.

Elizabeth looked at the girls, aching to take away their sadness, said, "Come here."

They came closer to where she was sitting. She put her arms around both and said, "It was only a dream. Your daddy is all right or we would have heard. Now we must get to our work."

## Chapter Thirteen

Back at Qumran, word spread rapidly about John's arrest and Philip's leaving. His meal mates and cave mates did their best to keep him from being depressed. His fellow-scriveners bade him a fond farewell. The two men—Amiel and Maaziah—in whose care he had been during the period of his incapacity bagged food they would need. They were keeping the dietary rule of the compound: to eat nothing that was not prepared by their priests. The wagon was filled with hay for the donkey's food, which would be used for Philip's bed. At last the time came to go. After farewells at the kitchen door, Philip—on his pallet—was lifted into the cart, and the two men walked toward the crest, leading the donkey. As they were about to leave the plateau, Aaron called, "Hold up!"

Looking back, they saw him running to catch them. He was carrying Philip's white robe. "Here's your robe. You will be wanting it when you get home."

"Oh! Thank you so much. Sorry that I am not going to be here long enough to be accepted as a full member." Reluctant to make the final break he prolonged the moment by saying, "If you or any of your emissaries are in Bethsaida, please know you will be most welcome to lodge at my family's home."

"Thank you, Philip. We shall always keep a bridge of friendship between us. And...remember...the day will come when you will receive a healing. Shalom, my friend."

With that the wagon party started out again. Looking back at the compound, Philip could see the men waving to him, a lump came to his throat. He was feeling that the important days in his life were made up of saying, "Goodbye".

They followed the same route down to the river they had used just four days before. As they approached the Jordan, Philip wished that he could hear John's voice once more preaching as he did the day before that horrible thing happened. Travelers were resting in the location, probably just as they had been since the time of Abraham. So Philip's party joined them. The heat of the afternoon was such that not many ventured out in the full sun. Philip re-lived the arrest scene he had witnessed, and wished time would pass so they could move on. After the sun lowered behind the hills on the western bank, the party pulled out. About three hours later they found another spot to stop for the night.

Philip's traveling companions were not talkative. Any exchange was pleasant, but brief—no unnecessary verbiage. The evening of the fourth day found them at the south end of the Sea of Galilee. Philip wondered: *Is Nathaniel fishing in the area tonight?* But he saw no boat close enough to hail. The next day they would follow the road up the east side of the lake until they came to Bethsaida. They should arrive at his father's house well before sundown, when Sabbath began. Philip was beginning to feel some excitement about seeing his loved ones again. He wondered: *how much have my daughters grown and changed? Will they know me?*

The road to Bethsaida wasn't as well traveled as the main road through the Jordan Valley. The little party met very few people, and none passed them. The path they were following kept to the level area of the lakeshore. Suddenly, Amiel, the priest walking by the donkey, stopped the animal. Philip, whose view was of that which they had passed—not what was ahead, wondered why the cessation of forward movement. The priest said softly, "Look ahead."

Philip turned his body so he could see. A small herd of antelope had come to the water's edge for a drink.

"What beautiful animals!" Philip exclaimed quietly. Many species of wild animals were in the hills, but the traveling party had not seen any this close. They were happy not having to deal with most of them: bears, lions or leopards. Jackals and wolves would have been bad enough. Other wild animals were of the deer or goat families.

"Let's rest here for awhile, and enjoy the view," said Maaziah. So the donkey was led to the water. Amiel dipped some water into a jar and brought it to Philip to drink. After dipping water for themselves, the priests seated themselves on the lakeshore, in the shade of the wagon, so they could observe the herd of antelope. This small act on the part of his companions gave Philip an insight to their sensitivity. They would delay their own trip so as not to disturb the wild animals' need for water.

The breeze from the lake made traveling bearable during the afternoon hours. The party reached

Bethsaida about two hours before sundown, these being the days preceding Rosh Hashanah, when daylight and dark were about equal in length. Philip directed the priests to his father's house.

As they approached the house, two little girls came running out the door and down the street shouting, "Abba! Abba! We knew you were coming!"

Philip's spirits lifted when he heard those young voices calling. The men smilingly stopped the donkey, and Philip said, "Can you come up here with me?"

With that invitation they grabbed hold of the wagon and climbed in with Philip. With Prisca on one side and Phoebe on the other, he hugged them both at the same time. "Sit here in the hay with me while we ride to the house."

"We knew you were coming home, Abba," Phoebe said.

"How did you know?"

Prisca answered, "Phoebe and I dreamed it! We saw you coming home in this wagon. But we don't know what is wrong with your legs."

Phoebe's big, innocent, brown eyes looking at him asked, "What is the matter with your legs, Abba?".

"Do you know what 'paralyzed' means?"

"No," they chimed together.

"Well, that means that I can't move them just by deciding that they should move. I have to pick them up with my hands, or be picked up by someone else."

With that they were at the courtyard door of his father's house. His parents, Jacob and Mary, brother Elias, his wife Sarah and their child, brother Nathaniel, his wife Elizabeth, and Philip's three-year-old daughter, Ruth, were waiting in the street.

82

The wagon party came to a stop. The family gathered around the end of the cart. As Philip saw the dear, familiar faces a lump came in his throat. He reached for the embrace of his father who said, "Welcome home, son." He couldn't answer immediately.

The little girls jumped out of the wagon. "His legs are...paralyzed." Phoebe said, carefully enunciating the word.

Prisca added, "That means he can't move them."

Jacob looked at Philip, "What's this?" he asked softly.

Philip nodded. His two companions were waiting at the edge of the family gathering. Jacob continued to stare at his son, not wanting to accept the news, as Philip said, "I want you to meet two of the best man-handlers I have ever known. They are Amiel and Maaziah, priests from Qumran. They will be with us for the Sabbath."

Jacob went to the men, salaamed to each, and said, "Thank you for being so kind to my son. Welcome to our home." Elias and Nathaniel followed as Philip spoke their names.

Each of the men nodded in return.

Jacob said, "Let's get you out of that wagon, and all of us inside." Philip's companions lifted him on his bed-pallet out of the wagon and followed Jacob into the courtyard. There he was put on the earthen floor. Elias and Nathaniel watched carefully how the men handled Philip and themselves so as to simplify movement and strain. They knew they would be responsible for lifting Philip from that time forward.

Philip addressed his mother, "The men have brought food from Qumran. You will not have to be concerned about your Sabbath preparations being enough."

"Oh, son!" Turning to the two men she said, "We always have more than enough."

"But they want to conform to their pledge to the Qumran discipline and eat only food prepared by their priests."

"Oh! ... I understand."

"All three of us want to bathe before the Sabbath begins."

"We will provide you with the means right away."

Basins of water were brought in and the women and children left the courtyard. As they departed Elizabeth said, "Children, let's bring the donkey and wagon in with our animals."

Jacob, Elias and Nathaniel stayed with Philip. They tried to visit with the companions. The two men were polite but they said nothing to encourage conversation. Nathaniel helped Philip to bathe. As he did so, Philip briefly told of the paralysis, how they had witnessed John's arrest, and of the trip to Bethsaida. The baths ended, towels were given to each man. Philip put on his white robe for the first time since surrendering it at Qumran. They finished dressing just as the sun dipped below the horizon and Sabbath had begun.

A typical Sabbath eve followed. As village priest, Jacob preceded his family to the synagogue to sound three sharp blasts on a ram's horn. This was the signal for which the villagers were waiting to go to the synagogue for prayer. Amiel and Maaziah, without a word, picked up Philip's bed and carried him to the synagogue with the rest of the family. It was a short distance—not any farther than when they carried him from the scriptorium to his cave.

After shocked surprise at seeing Philip on a litter, his friends and former students at the synagogue greeted him in gladness and warmth.

He was not prepared for the emotional reaction when he saw Hannah's parents, Mica and Zipporah. Mica looked tired and old beyond his years. Philip felt faint and would have collapsed if he weren't already seated on his pallet. His youngest daughter was walking! He could hardly believe his eyes. She was a miniature copy of Hannah. He saw his mother talking to Zipporah, so he knew the information of his returning home was being passed. They came to where he was seated. Mica dropped to his knees to embrace him, saying, "Welcome home, son. We're sorry to learn of your paralysis. Let us know what we can do to be of help."

"Thank you, Father. How is my little girl?"

With that little Esther was brought to stand before her father. "This is your abba, Esther," Mica said.

She somberly stared at the man in front of her, and then shyly hid her face in the robes of her grandmother. "She is doing just fine. She is starting to say a few words we can understand," Zipporah laughingly said.

"I am truly grateful that you have cared for her."

"It has been our joy," Zipporah replied.

The welcome made Philip glad that he had made the decision to come back. The women and girls separated themselves to their area, leaving the main floor of the synagogue for the men and boys. Evening prayers were over in an hour, and the villagers returned to their homes.

A meal for the whole family followed, with special foods that had been prepared ahead of time. Mica, Zipporah, and Esther had been invited to Jacob's home, as well as Philip's two sisters, their husbands and children. Amiel and Maaziah joined in the recitation of the Kiddush, a blessing over the wine, but they ate of the food and wine they had brought with them. Philip enjoyed being surrounded by his four daughters, and all of his family. During the meal, he was told the happenings in all their lives while he had been gone.

Eventually, the evening ended. The guests went home, and Jacob's household went to bed. Philip, Amiel and Maaziah slept in the courtyard. Philip realized that would probably be his permanent room. As he drifted off to sleep, he thought: *I will have to devise a tent to use during rainy weather.*

No trouble sleeping that night.

The next day was spent by going to the synagogue for prayer and scripture reading during the morning hours, and resting in the afternoon. Philip was again shocked when he saw his parents-in-law in the synagogue at how much Mica had aged and how tired he looked. He thought: *I am not the only one affected by Hannah's death.*

Jacob went to the synagogue at sunset and blew another signal on the ram's horn indicating the end of the Sabbath. Nathaniel left to put his fishing boat out for a night's catch.

Sunrise the next morning found Amiel and Maaziah, their donkey and wagon headed back to Qumran. They had arisen at dawn and quietly harnessed the animal to the cart. Philip sadly thanked them and bade them farewell. *Another goodbye*, he thought.

## Chapter Fourteen

Jacob's household was awakening when Zipporah came running to the courtyard door. Throwing it open wide, she ran into the yard crying, "I need help quickly. Mica won't...wake up!"

Philip's paralysis had never been so frustrating as it was at that moment.

If only I could jump up and run to him, he thought.

"Father! Elias!" he shouted.

One by one the whole family came running down the stairs. Zipporah sobbed, "Come quickly...I can't get Mica to wake up!"

Jacob, Elias, Mary and Sarah, Elias' wife, along with Zipporah, hurried toward Mica's house, which was close by. Philip, Elizabeth and the children were left at home.

Nothing could arouse Mica—he had died in his sleep. Tradition mandated that burial take place before the sun set. Jacob notified Mica's brother, who lived in the same village. The brother, as the only male in Mica's family, beat the drum, selected the burial location, and arranged the funeral procession.

Philip did not go to the funeral because of his disability. The two youngest children stayed with him. Even under the sad circumstances, he enjoyed watching their antics, but depression was creeping in on him. *Another farewell: I am responsible for Mica's death, just as surely as I was for Hannah's, he thought. I know he died of a broken heart. Why can't I just die, too?*

Philip selected a corner of the courtyard for his permanent bedroom. He had a tentmaker sew a high canopy slanting toward the outside wall. Falling rain would not be a problem.

The month of mourning for Mica crept by, one long day after another. Near the end of the period, Zipporah approached Philip as he sat on his pallet in the courtyard. "I would like to talk business with you, if I may."

"Please be seated." She placed a carpet and sat cross-legged on it so Philip could face her. She was a tall, stately built woman, but limber as a much younger woman. Philip was watching her facial expressions very intently.

"Mica's brother, Hiram, has made an offer for the property," and she mentioned the sum. "I am asking for your advice. Shall I accept it?"

"If you sell, where will you live?"

"Oh!" Looking away and then turning again to face Philip, "I thought you probably knew…Jacob and Mary have asked me to come here and live. Would that be all right with you?" She anxiously studied his face.

A smile softened Philip's sad countenance. "I would be pleased to have you here, to be a grandmother to all of the girls. You know Hannah's dying wish was to have you and Mica raise our daughters. She said you knew how to do it. She was going to teach them how to read and write."

"Yes, I know. If you wish, I would consider it an honor and a pleasure to fulfill Hannah's request."

"Do you know how?" After blurting it out, he thought *that's a stupid question*, but he hadn't known that Zipporah was literate.

"Yes, my father taught me. I, too, was an only child."

"I had thought that I would teach them, myself, but I would appreciate it if you would...you will have more time with them. Father is going to have the youngest boys come here for classes, and my time will be taken with them."

She demurely looked down as she answered, "I shall be glad to." Then, straightening her shoulders, she said, "Now, about the offer. Shall I sell? Since Mica had no male heirs, the property will go to Hiram anyway, when I die. If I sold, I would have some money to help with expenses here, and Hiram's son would have a place of his own."

"It sounds like an ideal arrangement, Mother. My advice is to accept the offer."

"Thank you." She smiled as she continued, "I was hoping that's what you would say. I'll send word to Hiram." She stood to leave.

At the end of the mourning period Zipporah and Esther moved into Philip and Hannah's room. Zipporah started teaching the girls in their room during the time Philip was holding class for the boys in the courtyard. Prisca and Phoebe were avid students, eager to learn. Ruth wanted to be doing that which her older sisters were doing, but her attention span was much shorter. Zipporah would break up the lessons with games that were also lessons of life. Little Esther was content to play by herself, inasmuch as she had lived without the daily companionship of sisters.

It eased Philip's mind to have the girls all together, and to be carrying out Hannah's dying request as well as he could.

## Chapter Fifteen

"Get down those stairs!" commanded one of the soldiers that had led John away from the Jordan.

John said, "I can't see where to go…it's too dark."

Another of the guards said, "I'll get a torch."

While they waited, John asked, "What is this place?"

"Machaerus."

John knew they had traveled southeast from the river, and had climbed to a great height, but he had never been here before.

The trip had taken all afternoon and into the night. While it was light enough to see, the peacefulness of Lake Asphaltitus was visible intermittently on the right. As they climbed higher, more of the surrounding countryside came into view. They didn't stop often, but when they did John could see the lush greenery of the Jordan Valley behind them contrasting with the beige barrenness of the wilderness on both sides of the river. Snow-capped Mount Hermon was clearly visible to the north.

Blue shadows deepened the ravines as dusk fell. John was sorry when darkness deprived him of seeing any more new features on the landscape of his homeland. When the soldiers stopped to eat an evening meal, John's hands were freed to eat from what he had in his sack. The disciples who followed kept a short distance away.

"What kind of a place is Machaerus?" John asked.

"It was an old fortress that was destroyed by Pompey's general. When Herod the Great rebuilt it, he put a palace inside it. Antipas spends much of his time here."

John knew they were behind a wall, because the sentry on duty at the gate challenged them. He could see in the dim light of the stars that the wall was higher and thicker than the one at Qumran. And the building into which he had been taken was made with bigger blocks of stone. He supposed his destination was a dungeon prison.

"Is he here now?"

"Yes. We go where he goes."

"How soon will I have a hearing?"

"That's not for us to say."

The soldier came with a torch and a jar with water and led the way down the stairs. The musty smell of an unventilated cellar was strong as he went deeper into the dungeon. The coolness of the stone steps could be felt through his sandals and was balm to his tired feet. By the light of the torch he could see a corridor with barred cells on each side. He was taken to the one closest to the stairway. His hands and feet were freed. The jar of water was left with him, and he was locked in. He could see a basin and a big pot in the cell before the soldiers took the torch and left. No sound of other prisoners was heard. John was alone with his God.

It was too dark for him to wash himself thoroughly—he didn't want to risk upsetting the water jar. Carefully feeling for the basin, he brought it close to the water container. He tilted the jug over and, listening to the sound of a trickle of water going into the basin, poured some into it. He wet his hands and rubbed them over his face. While saying his evening prayer and lifting his rich baritone voice to chant a psalm before lying down on the earthen floor, he knew he would have no trouble sleeping.

John awakened to a dark room. He knew morning had come; he could hear the shrill call of a bird coming from someplace outside. His eyes were by now accustomed to the dim light, and he saw one very small window near the door at the head of the long stairway. As the day grew lighter, he was able to see that he was in a big dungeon divided into cells with iron bars buried in building boulders in the ground and into planks in the ceiling. He tried to orient his body to face what he thought should be the direction of the rising sun to say his morning prayer.

Food was going to be a problem, if he were going to remain here more than a few days. He knew he would not eat even if the guards brought him meals, and he didn't have much left in his sack. *I shall not need much food while I am here,* he thought. So, he rationed himself a small handful of dried berries he had picked several weeks before at the peak of their season.

"I have taken a vow to eat only the food that I harvest myself, or that which is prepared by the priests at Qumran," John said when the guard, a very young man, later brought him food. He hesitated, and then brightly added, "You look like you could use a little more food. You eat it."

The guard, unused to being given anything, was in a quandary. It was true: he was always hungry; he could eat it and no one else need know. But, was it something over which he could get into trouble, if it were known? He took it away staring at him as if he questioned John's sanity. But before he left the dungeon, he sat on the steps to eat the food.

"May I know your name, son?" John tenderly asked the guard.

"Hasshub."

"Hasshub. That's an honorable name. Are you a Levite?"

"Yes."

"Did you know that a Hasshub joined with Nehemiah in signing the covenant to keep the Law?"

Taking a bite of food, he said, "Yes. How do you know so much?"

"I was trained to be a priest."

The guard stopped chewing and stared at John in disbelief, giving the food in his mouth a couple more chews, then gulped it down. "What are you doing in prison?"

"I assume that Antipas took exception to my calling him and his mistress adulterers."

Hasshub inhaled audibly. In a surprised voice he stated more than asked, "You ... you're John the baptizer!"

"I am John, and I baptize."

With awe, he said, "I have heard about you."

"Is that so?"

"Oh, yes!" He kept staring at John. Hesitating, he said, "From what I am told, it was probably Herodias' doing more than Antipas to have you arrested." Hasshub paused as if he had said too much.

John, completely puzzled, said, "That's very interesting. Now the question is why?"

"Well, he is usually fair-minded, but...she is a witch."  After a moment's hesitation, smiling, he continued, "She has a beautiful daughter, though."

"Oh?  How old is the daughter?"

"I'd guess...fourteen or fifteen."

"Who is her father?"

"Antipas' half-brother...Herod the Great's son who was disinherited."

"What is her name?"

"Salome."

"Is she here now?"

"Yes.  Barrack gossip has it that Antipas is more bewitched now by Salome than by Herodias."

"Oh?"  John hesitated, "Well, that is very interesting."

Suddenly embarrassed that he had been sharing loose talk with a prisoner, and enjoying it, Hasshub said, "I must leave."  He stood and turned to climb the stairs.

"It's been nice meeting you, Hasshub.  You are a very intelligent young man.  I hope we will meet again."

He started to answer; instead he climbed the stairs, unlocked the door at the top, went through it and locked it behind him, but....

Hasshub's bringing food to John and sitting on the steps to eat it while talking with him became routine.

John spent his days speaking aloud the scriptures he had learned by memory as a small boy, and chanting the psalms.  He put himself on one meal a day that consisted of a few berries or a date.  He thought:

*God was looking after me when he provided me with
so many berries to harvest and dry.*

After a few days, John said to Hasshub, "Who do I
need to talk to about having a hearing before Antipas?"

"I don't know. I'll try to find out."

The next time Hasshub came he said, "My superior
said he would inquire of Antipas' Chief Scribe about
holding your hearing."

"Well, thank you, Hasshub. I hope it didn't create
an awkward situation for you."

"No, not at all. By the way, some friends of yours
are camped outside the gates. They would like to see
you, but my superior denies their request."

John, as big and strong as he had ever been, was
thankful that Hasshub was unable to see the tears in his
eyes. When composure allowed a controlled voice, he
said, "That's nice to know...that I have friends who
are interested in what...happens to me."

"Oh! From what I've heard, your teachings have
reached all over the kingdom, and you have followers
in far away places."

"Really?"

"Yes. I thought you knew."

"No, I didn't. My temple was the rest area at the
crossroad by the Jordan, and travelers were coming or
going from all over. It pleases me to hear that,
Hasshub. It really does. Maybe my life hasn't been in
vain, after all, praise God. Praise God, I say."

For two days Hasshub had no news regarding
John's hearing. The third day he said, "My superior
said to tell you that Antipas is leaving Machaerus to go
to another of his palaces for awhile. He will hold your
hearing when he returns."

"When will that be?"

"No one knows. He usually comes here for his birthday. He has a big party and invites notables and dancing girls for entertainment. But that will not be for several months."

John grabbed hold of the bars, shaking them. Hasshub jumped back.

"Several months? Starvation will eliminate the need! What good is a hearing for a dead man?" The old anger was aroused in strong strides of resentment.

Hasshub was starting up the stairs. His youthfulness had not prepared him for the abrupt change of personality in a man. John called after him, "See if you can get word to Antipas so I can get this over with. I still have work that needs doing."

Hasshub hastily made his exit. The gentle man he had gotten to know was not this wild person.

The next delivery of John's food Hasshub was unusually mute. Muffled sounds of soldiers shouting and horses pulling heavy wagons penetrated the thick walls. John knew that Antipas and his retinue were departing. Momentarily he felt desolate. But then he remembered that he was in God's hands and said aloud, "Not as I desire, but grant me the courage to fulfill my mission."

A small contingent of soldiers remained at the fortress. Hasshub was among them.

Machaerus was located at an elevation high enough to see sections of the important north-south road from the Red Sea to Damascus. It was near the border of Antipas' area of authority. Foreign aggression was always expected. The father of Antipas' first wife,

King Aretas of Petra, was very unhappy with Antipas' divorcing of his daughter. They also had quarreled over the boundary limits of their countries. The soldiers guarded the fortress itself from plunderers and Jewish Zealots who were looking for ways to overthrow Rome, the true power in the known world. Herod Antipas was allowed to have his kingdom, as a son of Herod the Great, but he had to stay in favor with Tiberius Caesar.

## Chapter Sixteen

"People were commenting at the synagogue this morning about a new rabbi that is going about the countryside teaching and preaching. Do you know him?" Philip asked his brothers Elias and Nathaniel while resting, one Sabbath afternoon.

"No," Elias answered, "but he is gathering quite a following. Do you remember Simon Bar-Jonah and his brother Andrew?"

"Fishermen, aren't they?" Philip asked.

"Yes. They have started following the rabbi."

Nathaniel added, "I heard that James and John, sons of Zebedee, and another Philip from our village have joined his group, too, and are camp followers."

"I know all of them. What is he teaching that is attracting people like that?"

"I don't know. I haven't gone out to hear him," Elias replied.

Nathaniel said, "Neither have I, but my friends said he told Simon and Andrew that he would make them fishers of men."

"Do you know his name?"

"They call him 'Y'shua.'"

A shiver ran down Philip's spine. An image of the visitor at Qumran came to his mind's eye. The quickening of flesh told him this man Y'shua was not the usual rabbi.

## Chapter Seventeen

John's food ran out. Each day found him weaker. He had no spare fat on his body to start with, but now he was beginning to look gaunt. Loose skin hung that had been taut covering muscle. Cheekbones took on more prominence as the fleshy part of his cheeks sunk in. His eyes were beginning to bulge. Each day he lost more strength.

Antipas had been gone a week when behind Hasshub, as he came through the door and down the stairs, were two men in white robes. John thought: *am I seeing things? Have I started having visions?* Then he recognized Amiel and Maaziah from Qumran.

Hasshub said, "I brought some visitors to see you."

John's weakness caused an emotion of tearful happiness, and he couldn't trust his voice to respond. He put his arms through the bars and embraced each man.

Amiel said, "We witnessed your arrest, and were told of your being left here without a hearing. Our priest-cook, Jesse, learned that you did not bring much food with you, so he sent us to you with a supply."

Maaziah added, "We have our garden wagon full of foodstuff for you."

John's amazement at this life-saving turn of events led him to real tears. His voice choked as he said, "Praise God...from whom...all blessings flow! Did you say you witnessed my arrest…how did that happen?"

The men then related how they had taken Philip down to John at the Jordan arriving just in time to see him arrested and taken away.

"I'm sorry. Philip may have received a healing. Some people did after repenting. If Philip's paralysis is caused by his sins, or something he considers sin, he may have been healed. How did you learn of my present difficulty?"

"You have disciples. Some are camped outside the fortress. We saw them when we came in. One visited us at Qumran, and let us know of your circumstances."

"Praise God. I didn't know they were still here. How are Aaron, and everyone at Qumran?"

"Life goes on about the same. Maaziah and I went to Bethsaida. We took Philip home," said Amiel.

Maaziah added, "On the way back we heard that a new rabbi is drawing quite a following from the Galilee area."

"We were told that he is going all over the countryside healing, preaching, and teaching," Amiel said.

John inhaled, paused, and cautiously asked, "Do you know his name?"

"Yes. It is Y'shua. He was a visitor at Qumran just before you left. Do you remember him?"

"Yes. I know him." John said reflectively and hesitated, "Do you…think …he is the Messiah?"

"We doubt it, but time will tell," Amiel quickly replied.

Hasshub had remained in the background listening, but now he stepped forward. "It is time to start bringing in the supplies."

"All right," Amiel answered.

"I'll get some soldiers to help," and Hasshub followed the priests up the stairs.

John was surprised at the amount and variety of food they brought. Hasshub opened the door and it was stashed in his cell. The tanner had sent a skin blanket, and some of the dray donkey's hay was left to give John a softer bed.

The cell door was still open and they were all inside the enclosure. He invited Amiel and Maaziah to sit on the ground and share as John broke some bread and cheese and opened a bottle of wine. He said to Hasshub, "Will you and your friends join us? If it weren't for you, these men would not be in here."

Hasshub looked at the three other soldiers, all of who were about the same age as Hasshub. He answered, "We'll have a drink from your bottle is all."

John asked God's blessing on the food. As they ate John said, "Thank you so much for bringing me all this, and be sure to give my love and appreciation to Aaron, Jesse, and the others."

When they finished eating, each said, "Goodbye, John," and embraced him. Both of the men could feel his bones, realizing how much weight John had lost. John answered, "Shalom."

## Chapter Eighteen

"All she does is play with the girls!" Sarah, wife of Philip's brother Elias, said to Elizabeth, wife of Nathaniel, as they were grinding meal into flour in the courtyard.

Zipporah, Philip's mother-in-law, was being absorbed into a household organized by his mother, Mary, and it had not been too easy.

"I miss having the girls with me.. They are such a delight to teach." Elizabeth responded.

Philip was holding class in his corner of the yard, but was overhearing the complaints of his sisters-in-law. He was pleased with the progress Zipporah was making in teaching his girls. The twins were already starting to read the Torah, memorizing it as they learned the words.

"What I would like to know is what good will it do those girls to be able to read and write? It will not help them to get husbands!" This came from Sarah.

"Well, I don't think it will hurt to have the ability...I wish that I could...but they are missing out on training in all these other duties that they must know to be good wives and mothers," Elizabeth replied.

"Half a day isn't enough time." Sarah said this because Zipporah released the children from scholarly pursuits each afternoon. Ruth, the 3-year-old, and Esther, the youngest, took naps, but the twins, Prisca and Phoebe, were eager to be with their substitute mother, Elizabeth.

"Daughters," Mary said. She had been a silent co-worker with the women. "We have been over this before. We are just going to have to reconcile ourselves to the situation for the time being. In all my years of living, if there is anything I have learned, it is that nothing is permanent. Change will come eventually, whether we want it or expect it. Change will come."

"Yes, Mother."

Philip breathed a sigh of relief, and silently thanked his mother and her wisdom. Sitting in the courtyard, day after day teaching the little boys, he had become a fixture for the women. He grew tired of their chatter. They ignored his presence after the first couple of weeks, and talked about anything. For instance, he knew Elizabeth was pregnant before her husband did. He knew he should be happy for them, but he could find very little joy within himself.

His mother's philosophy that nothing is permanent was just wishful thinking to his state of mind. It appeared that he was permanently paralyzed. All his efforts to be healed were wasted energy. If only he could go back and relive his last year with Hannah, and control his desires for her—he missed her so much.

The depression he was in caused him actual pain. It was only with much effort that he maintained a friendly relationship with the members of his family and friends. His inclination was to withdraw within himself and not talk to anyone.

## Chapter Nineteen

John could hardly believe what had actually happened. But a supply of food was there in the corner of his cell. It should last a long time—maybe even the "several months" until Antipas' birthday. He had thought his work on earth was finished and he was prepared to die from starvation. *God must have something more for me to do. It could have been my imagination that day at the river when I baptized Y'shua. I wish I knew for sure that he is the Messiah. Then I would know if my work is complete or if I need to try to escape to continue my preaching.*

At that moment Hasshub came through the door and down the stairs. John said, "I want to thank you, Hasshub, for making it possible that my brothers from Qumran could come inside and bring me this food."

"My superior said that as long as you are going to be here until Antipas comes back, you may have visitors, but not more than two at a time."

"Praise God! Another answer to an unspoken prayer! Please tell your superior that I am grateful. I'm too tired today to see anyone else, but tomorrow may I see two of those who are outside the fortress?"

"I'll send the word." He hesitated. "Um, when you are stronger, will you tell me...what you were preaching?"

John looked at Hasshub's young, handsome face and clung desperately to maintain his composure.

Here, in a filthy, dungeon prison behind bars, God wants me to preach the word to this young man. Finally, he said, "My dear, gentle, young friend it will be my pleasure. What about the other soldiers… would they like to be part of my congregation?"

Hasshub's face brightened and a full smile beamed across it as he said, "I don't know, but I'll ask them."

The next day two of John's disciples were brought into the dungeon prison. It took a little time for their eyes to adjust to the darkness. When they could make out his figure, they were shocked at the sight of him. If they didn't know it was John, they would not have recognized him. Shyness kept them back.

John called out, "Shalom, my friends. I am told that you have been camped outside the fortress since I was taken prisoner. May I know your names?"

"Mine is Phinehas, and his is Segub."

"How have you managed to camp up here for so long?"

They came a little closer to the cell. Phinehas answered, "We take turns going home for supplies. Some are in camp all the time, but not everybody."

"How many are there of you?"

After a moment's hesitation, Segub said, "We total about 24, I guess."

John, still quite weak, slowly nodded, and said, "How nice. And what do you do while you are up here?"

"We pray for your release. We repeat to each other your teachings," Segub said.

John remembered that sometimes he thought he had heard people singing in the distance, but wasn't sure. He asked, "What news have you heard from Galilee or the Jordan Valley?"

Phinehas said, "Everything is about the same."

Segub added, "A new rabbi is going around the Sea of Galilee and getting quite a following, we hear."

John thought: *Here it is again. It must be. It has to be.* "What is he teaching?"

"We haven't heard him."

"Do you think he might be the Messiah?"

"We don't know."

"How soon will either one of you be going home?"

Phinehas said, "We travel together. We had planned to leave tomorrow." He hesitated and then asked, "Why?"

John felt compelled to know for sure. "Would it be possible for you to find this new rabbi and ... and ask him a question for me?"

Both paused, looked at each other, and nodded before Phinehas said, "Yes, I think we can. Our homes are in Capernaum. He seems to be making one of the homes there his headquarters. It should be no problem to locate him. What is the question?"

John thought: *how best to word the question so they won't get it wrong.* Hesitating, he said, "Ask him for me, ... 'Are you the one who is to come, or shall we look for another?'"

Phinehas and Segub thought on the meaning of John's question he wanted them to ask.

John looked at them very intently. They repeated the question in unison, "Are you the one who is to come, or shall we look for another."

John said more to himself than to the men, "Yes. That is my question." He continued, "Please listen very carefully to what he says. I want to hear his answer...word for word."

Phinehas said, "We consider it an honor to carry your question and return with his reply. We're happy to be able to...do something for you."

Segub, seeing that John was tiring, spoke, "We had better leave now."

John said, "Thank you ever so much for coming to see me...for keeping the vigil outside the walls...for sending someone to Qumran, and for taking my message to the rabbi." As he reached through the bars to take each by his hand, said, "Let us pray together: The Lord bless you and keep you. The Lord make his face to shine upon you and be kind to you. The Lord put his countenance upon you, and to give you peace. Amen."

# Chapter Twenty

A local businessman, Ishi, approached Philip one Sabbath at the synagogue.  Ishi, an unusually quiet man, said as he nervously rubbed his prayer beads, "May I call on you tomorrow afternoon?"

"Yes.  Father and I will be home," Philip replied. Inasmuch as Jacob and Philip wrote letters and contracts for the villagers, it was not unusual to have a businessman make an appointment to call on them. However, business affairs were never conducted on a Sabbath, and Ishi's behavior was abnormal for someone who just wanted a letter written.  Philip couldn't help but be intrigued by his motive.

A knock on the courtyard door the next afternoon was answered by Jacob, "Come in, Ishi!"

"Shalom, Jacob," he said as he bowed slightly and entered the courtyard.

"What can we do for you?" Jacob asked.

"I thought that I should talk to Philip, but perhaps I need to talk to you, too."

Philip said, "Father and I have very few differences."

"That makes it nice," Ishi said, as he looked around the courtyard.  The women and older children were outside in the garden; the younger children were napping, Elias was in the field, and Nathaniel was in his room upstairs taking his rest.

"Yes. Come sit with us, Ishi, and speak freely," invited Philip. He and his father did their letter writing while seated on the ground, using a low table for support of their scrolls.

Ishi put one foot behind the other and sat down, crossing his ankles. He was a man about the age of Jacob—early fifties, graying dark hair and beard, dark brows and brown eyes. He was tall and had the bearing of a man of importance. They knew him to be a sincere, gentle man, fair in all his dealings. Today he was not at ease. As far as Philip could remember, he had never married.

Jacob said, "Would you enjoy some wine?"

"Oh, thank you, Jacob…I would."

Jacob brought three cups and a bottle of wine. Rarely did the family drink wine other than with special meals. Giving the bottle to Philip, he said, "Would you pour?"

As Philip poured the wine Jacob said, "I'll get some bread and cheese.

They go well with the wine."

"That's very nice, Jacob. Thank you," Ishi replied.

Jacob brought the bread, broke off three chunks, put them on a plate with the hard cheese. He then took a seat on the floor.

Each one took a piece of bread and a portion of the cheese, and sipped the wine. Ishi said, "Very good wine. Do you make it yourself?"

Jacob answered, "No, we barter for it. We have eggs and butter that Mary trades for things that we do not have."

Ishi cleared his throat and said, "I suppose you are wondering why I have come here this afternoon."

Philip said, "It is pleasant to have you call, but I sense that you have something else on your mind."

"Yes, I do. It has taken a lot of courage for me to reach this stage for you see, I am a shy man." He paused. Philip nodded for him to continue. "I have a good business and am successful because I tend to it like a shepherd. But I have never married because of...my shyness. Now," he hesitated, then rushing ahead as though he felt that since he had started he didn't want to quit until he had said it all, "Now, I have decided to ask Philip, or you, Jacob, for permission to marry Zipporah." He hurriedly added, "I have a nice home and can provide her with a comfortable life."

Philip, for the first time in a long time, wanted to laugh. He glanced at Jacob, who was struggling to keep his composure, too. After a moment's silence, Philip soberly said, "Ishi, I think Zipporah would consider it a privilege to be asked to be your wife, but she can speak for herself. Is that not so, Father?"

"Yes, Ishi. Mica's brother, Hiram, had first chance to marry her, but he can't afford more than one wife. He bought the property from her for his son, which...legally...he did not have to do. He could have taken it, dispossessed her and not given her anything."

Ishi said, "I have talked to Hiram. He is the one who said I needed to talk to Philip."

Philip said, "I am glad you came to me, Ishi, but Zipporah is free to make her own contracts. Father and I will advise her, but only if she asks. She is a fine woman, and will make you a good wife. She can help you in your business, too. She reads and writes."

"Yes, I know. I...I have had a lifelong attraction to Zipporah...perhaps that is the real reason that I never married. Mica's father spoke for her

before my father thought about it. Of course, she never knew how I felt, but living in the same community, I could see her now and then."

Suddenly Philip had a new appreciation for his mother-in-law. Not only had she been Mica's wife, Hannah's mother, and grandmother to his children— she had a secret admirer! He pictured her in his mind's eye: an attractive woman, although he wouldn't consider her beautiful. He saw how Ishi could desire her for his wife.

Jacob said, "If she should ask us, we will endorse you, Ishi. You can depend on that."

Ishi looked at Jacob, and then Philip. His serious expression changed into a broad, warm smile. "Thank you," he said, "You are both very kind."

At that moment the women and children, laughing and talking, came into the courtyard from the garden, each carrying a basket loaded with produce. When they saw that Jacob and Philip had a caller, they shushed the children and quietly put down their baskets.

Philip raised his voice, "Mother Zipporah, would you please come here?"

All the women and children looked to see who the visitor was. Zipporah's heart thumped. *It is Ishi!* From the time she was a teenager, when she first became aware of boys, she always felt this way when she saw him.

Zipporah walked toward the men. Mary, Sarah and Elizabeth stayed where they were. They would be able to hear everything, if they kept quiet.

"Shalom, Ishi," Zipporah said.

"Shalom, Zipporah."

Philip said, "Please sit down and join us. Ishi wants to ask you something."

Zipporah's heart leaped. Picking up a mat and seating herself on it on the earthen floor, heart racing, she calmly said, "What is it, Ishi?"

"Zipporah, I have tried going through Hiram and today through Philip or Jacob, but I am told that you are the one to whom I must talk."

"So, talk." Zipporah was feeling as shaky as a leaf, but knew she must keep her composure.

"I...I want to...marry you." Ishi hurriedly added, "I will give you a good home and any comfort you ask. I'm in excellent health."

Zipporah sat back with surprise. She looked first at Philip, and then Jacob, both of whom were smiling. She felt weak. She had to admit to herself that if she could choose a husband, Ishi would be her choice. Also, the thought of a marriage bed gave her a thrill; she had enjoyed—and missed—that part of married life. But other things needed to be considered.

"You honor me, Ishi. I thank you for asking me to be your wife. May I have some time to think it over?"

Ishi smiled and exhaled, as if he had been holding his breath, answered, "You honor me for considering my proposal. Could I show you my home and business, to acquaint you with what a life with me would be like?"

"Perhaps later. Let me first get used to the idea. Is that all right with you?" Zipporah replied.

"Oh, yes! I did not intend to rush you. But I'm pleased that you are going to give it thought. If it's all right with you, I shall call again in seven days."

"Seven days! … All right. I'll try to have an answer for you in seven days."

Ishi, standing, said, "Thank you, Jacob, for the wine. I must go now, but I shall return for an answer in seven days."

Zipporah and Jacob also stood. Philip could see that Ishi and Zipporah would make an outstanding-looking couple. Both were tall and stately. It seemed natural that they should be together as husband and wife.

"Go with God," Zipporah said as they bid farewell at the doorway of the courtyard.

## Chapter Twenty-one

John gained strength from the food brought by the priests from Qumran. The hollows in his cheeks began to fill out. The loose skin was beginning to fill out a little. He could breathe the foul air a bit better as he slowly regained his strength.

Soon a new routine was established. Hasshub and three other soldiers came to listen to John teach and preach each morning, the Sabbath being no exception. John thought: *Jehovah God moves in mysterious ways His miracles to perform.*

In the afternoon two disciples were allowed to come in and visit. He learned that they were deciding who would come by drawing lots among those who had not yet been in to see him. So different men were coming every day. He looked forward to meeting Zoheth, who had gone to Qumran, and thanking him. In the evening reciting scripture and chanting psalms, he also wondered what the answer to his question would be.

John waited impatiently for the return of Phinehas and Segub. His future hung on the answer they would bring.

He now knew that escape to continue his mission was possible; there would be no trouble from the guards, and assistance from his followers. He realized the guards would be in jeopardy of severe punishment and perhaps his friends in the camp, too.

Meanwhile, he felt somewhat like a priest again, being useful to God.

Eighteen days had passed since Phinehas and Segub had left. Others from the camp had told John that they usually returned within fourteen days. John thought: *perhaps they are having trouble in finding Y'shua.*

John's heart leapt in his chest for, indeed, the two visitors the next day were Phinehas and Segub. They seemed to glow with an aura of sunshine. *What was so different about them?*

"Shalom, my friends." Arising to a standing position, reaching through the bars of the cell, and grasping their hands in friendship, John continued, "I am happy to see that you have returned safely."

"Shalom," they both responded. Phinehas continued, "John, we have met the Messiah!"

John inhaled quickly, grabbing the bars with renewed strength. "Tell me, what proof do you have? Did you have trouble finding the rabbi? Is it Y'shua?"

"Yes…that is his name. We had no trouble finding him…" Phinehas hesitated.

Segub continued, "…Multitudes are following him. We had trouble just getting near enough to ask him your question,"

Phinehas said, "We witnessed so many healings, and listened to his preaching…"

"…We knew what the answer to your question would be!" Segub finished the statement.

John, just a little puzzled asked, "Then, you did get to ask him?"

"Oh, yes," they answered simultaneously.

John breathed a deep sigh of relief. "And what...exactly...did he say?"

Phinehas recited as though it had been rehearsed many times on their return trip, "Go and tell John what you see and hear: the deaf hear, the blind see..." John could feel excitement building from the pit of his stomach. "... the lame walk, lepers are cleansed..." John's heart started beating faster. "...the dead are raised up..." John is thinking: *he is the fulfillment of prophecies.*

When Phinehas paused, Segub picked up the recitation. "...and the poor have good news preached to them. And blessed is he who takes no offense at me."

"Did you actually see these miracles yourself?"

Segub said, "We saw many of them. We did not see the dead raised, but we were told about two children being restored to life."

"Tell me more. Tell me more. Every bit of it."

The two men stayed on, with Hasshub listening in the background, until they had related every detail of what they had heard and seen. Finally, John said, "My mission is finished. All he has done fulfills prophecy. He who I am unworthy of unfastening his sandals has come. You may tell my followers to go join the multitude and be his disciples. Thank you, my dear friends, and Shalom."

"We will not leave you. Shalom for now."

When he was alone John knelt to pray. "Oh, merciful God, I give thanks. I give thanks. I knew it. I knew it. This is not the way I planned on learning the news, but even as I am imprisoned here, You bring me this wonderful word. Thy will be done with my life. Amen."

The happiness John felt from knowing for certain that Y'shua was the long-awaited Messiah outweighed the emotion of emptiness he also was experiencing. He thought: *I must be content to teach the guards, and anyone else who can come within the small arena of my daily life. I am happy that I can now preach the Messiah has come, rather than a future event for which to be prepared. And — I have seen him! Not only in the flesh, but as part of the glow Phinehas and Segub actually have about them. I have actually known him all my life! And—here—in this dirty, stinking, dark cell I have received the greatest news of my life. Yes! Miracles do happen!*

## Chapter Twenty-two

Zipporah was alternately teased and loved by the women during the week that followed Ishi's proposal. This was a turn of events that no one—least of all Zipporah—had expected.

It was in the afternoon before the Sabbath was to begin, Zipporah asked Philip if they could talk. He invited her to sit with him. She sat on a mat, facing him. She said, "I need to know your feelings about Ishi's marriage proposal. My head has been in a whirl ever since he was here the other day."

"Before I say, tell me your inclination," Philip responded.

Zipporah hesitated. She looked down. *Was she ready to share how she really felt about him?* She carefully picked her words. "I...have always ...respected...Ishi." Looking up, she continued, "I feel highly flattered, of all the widows in town, he has chosen me."

After a pause, Philip asked, "Does it appeal to you to be married to him?"

Blushing, she glanced down and answered softly, "I can not deny that it does!" Then boldly looking Philip in the eye said, "If I had not liked the idea, I probably would have turned him down first off. But... what about the children and their lessons? And I need to know how you feel about it."

Reaching for her hand, Philip took it and covered it with his other one and said, "Mother Zipporah, I love you and want the very best in life for you. You are only 44 years old, in good health—you will live a long time. Being married to Ishi will give you a companionship into old age that grandchildren cannot provide. I want for you the same as you desire."

Before responding Zipporah thought, *he knows the loneliness of being without a wife—he understands my needs.* Withdrawing her hand, she asked, "You will not think that I am dishonoring Mica's memory if I remarry?"

"In your own heart will you be dishonoring him?" Philip mirrored back for her to examine her own attitude.

She looked away and paused before slowly answering, "My mother said to me as I was being prepared for marriage to Mica...I was not too happy over the arrangement...'We women do not marry the men we love, Zipporah. We love the men we marry.'" Turning to look at Philip again, she added, "And I did. He was a kind, gentle man, and I learned to love him."

Philip waited for her to continue, and when she didn't, he asked, "So your experience as a married woman was positive?"

"Yes...but I need to know how you feel."

"The way I look at it is this: you would be honoring Mica by taking another husband."

Zipporah sat up straight and stared back at Philip, "How so?"

"You liked your life with him so much that you wish to enter into married life again. I am sure Mica would approve…his lifelong desire was for your happiness, was it not?"

"Oh, yes! You are right…if I had not had a good marriage with Mica, I probably would never want to remarry." Hesitating, she asked, "What about the children and their lessons? They are doing so well, and I love teaching them."

"I would like for them to continue their lessons with you, too. You are going to be living here in the village. They can go to you, or you can come to them…whatever is best for you. Something can be worked out. It isn't an issue to stop you from marrying."

Smiling, she rose to her knees and said, "Thank you Philip. You have helped me very much. I'll take the twins this afternoon for a stroll to Ishi's place of business and accept his invitation to look at the house." She embraced him and kissed him on the cheek.

He returned her embrace. "My privilege, Mother."

A sense of worthiness cradled Philip's entire being. Shivers of a blessing from God traveled up his spine. He felt that he had been of real use and comfort to Zipporah, a beautiful soul.

Zipporah started to rise, then came down to her knees again. "Oh! One more thing…the money I brought with me when I came here. I have been contributing to the expense of the household from it, but I have a balance remaining…"

"That is yours, Mother. Every bride should have some money of her own."

"When I die, your daughters will inherit whatever balance is left."

"I appreciate your thoughtfulness, Mother. Thank you. But this is not the day to talk about dying! Go. Be happy."

"Shalom, Philip. Out of all the tragedy of the past...I have gained a wonderful son," she spoke as she rose to her feet and went in search of the twins.

Having reached the decision to follow her heart, Zipporah had trouble keeping it to herself until the day after the Sabbath when Ishi was to come for his answer. The women of the house knew her secret from the radiance of her smile and the sound of singing coming from her room. The friends she saw at the synagogue asked each other, "What has come over Zipporah?" Mary reminded her daughters-in-law that she had said change would come.

Finally came the afternoon of the day after the Sabbath. The women made a point of not going to the garden so they could be present. Elias and the children, too, found reasons to be in the courtyard. Nathaniel was the only one that day who was doing that which he routinely did, getting his rest.

When the knock came on the courtyard door, Jacob opened it wide, and greeted him with "Shalom, Ishi. Come in."

Ishi straightened with surprise by the courtyard being filled with so many members of the family. He mumbled, "Shalom," as he entered. He bowed slightly to Jacob and Elias, but looked at Zipporah and sought out her eyes. His heart pounded in his chest. *Was her smile one of acceptance, or to let him down easy?*

Jacob said, "Come, sit with us."

Ishi answered, "Thank you," as he sat on the earthen floor near Philip. Jacob and Elias both seated themselves.

Jacob said, "We know you did not come to see us." Turning, he said, "Zipporah, will you join us?"

She walked over, carrying a mat, putting it on the floor, and sitting down on it. "Shalom, Ishi." She looked into his eyes, and knew she had made the right decision. She felt he was reading her heart. Suddenly she felt weak, but told herself to be strong.

Ishi said softly, looking at Zipporah, "Today is when I get an answer to my proposal of marriage. What do you have to say?"

Zipporah answered in an unusually strong voice, "I feel honored to be asked to be your wife, Ishi. I intend to accept your offer..."

Ishi had been holding his breath, and he exhaled with a laugh. He then filled his lungs with air and exhaled slowly. With a broad smile, he said, "Thank you, Zipporah. You have just made me a very happy man."

"...I am not finished. Before these witnesses I wish to tell you...I will be bringing with me a sum of money left to me by Mica and from Hiram buying the house." She paused before continuing, "It is my will that when I die, the remaining funds should be kept in trust for my four granddaughters, in equal proportion."

"Fair enough! Since I have no relatives, and before these same witnesses, I will that they shall be my heirs, too. We shall put it in writing." He looked at Jacob, "Can we do it now?"

"Yes! Yes, I'll write it for your signatures." And Jacob reached for his papyrus scroll, quill and ink, and began to write. He had been taken aback at Zipporah's pre-marital financial arrangement.

Ishi, digging into a pouch, brought out a necklace of gold chain set with amethyst stones of the deepest purple. "I brought this for you, Zipporah, in the hope you would give me an affirmative reply."

Gasps escaped from all the women as they saw its beauty. Zipporah reached to take it, held it up to catch the light, and said, "It is lovely, Ishi. Thank you." The other women and girls gathered around to admire the necklace.

After signing the will, congratulations, embraces, handshakes were exchanged by all in the courtyard. Jacob said, "Let us enjoy some wine while we plan the wedding."

Ishi said to Zipporah, "We will not need a long betrothal, will we? We have known each other all our lives."

Zipporah replied, "All I need is time to prepare a garment worthy of the occasion! I shall look for fabric that will set off the beauty of the stones in the necklace."

# Chapter Twenty-three

Nearly ten months had passed since John's arrest. Hasshub told him that recently supplies had started arriving for the party. The crunch of wheels of heavy wagons in gravel announced the return of Antipas. When he heard the sound, a sensation of foreboding caused his heart to beat harder, and his breathing became shallow.

Two weeks of preparation for the party, and the return of the soldiers with Antipas, upset the daily routine John had grown accustomed to. The guards could no longer come in for a teaching, nor could his friends from outside the wall visit him. True to their word, Phinehas and Segub had remained faithful, but they had told the others of John's releasing them. Some had gone and not returned. John was once again alone with his God, reciting the scriptures and chanting psalms.

Hasshub came to see John during the afternoon before the party. He said, "John, I have just a few minutes. I wanted to see you and let you know that I feel privileged to have been able to sit at your feet and learn from you. While Antipas is here, we will not be able to come, but if you are still here when he goes, I hope to renew our lessons."

"Bless you, Hasshub. I have enjoyed having a class and your friendship. My mission was to prepare the way for the long-awaited Messiah. Now that he has come, my work is finished. I am ready for whatever Jehovah has for me. Is everything all set for the party?"

"Yes. The dancing girls are here." He hesitated, smiling, "The soldiers are enjoying their company. Friends and family members have been arriving the last two days. So the celebrating is underway. But the big banquet with plenty of wine and dancing is this evening. No one will sleep tonight, except you...maybe! Well, I must go. Shalom, John."

"May the Lord watch between you and me, while we are absent one from the other. Shalom."

"Amen."

## Chapter Twenty-four

"The bride is ready." Zipporah sent this message to Ishi about a month later via Elias and Nathaniel.

The women helped her to dress in the new wedding apparel: A satin brocade in a soft shade of light mauve banded at the lower edge and sleeves with embroidery matching the color of the stones in her necklace. A belt at the waist was also emblazoned with purple stitches. The necklace was fastened around her throat. A short veil was placed on her head and fastened with a garland of flowers from their garden.

As she descended the stairs into the courtyard, Philip had to blink to hold back the tears. *She is so radiantly beautiful!* And momentarily he had the illusion it was Hannah coming down the steps. He was so happy for Zipporah. He thought: *she is blessed by God to have two worthy men wish to share their lives with her, first Mica and now Ishi.*

"God bless you, Mother Zipporah," Philip said.

"Thank you, Philip. I cannot sit down. Not yet."

Philip reached up and took her hand, "You are a lovely bride. I wish you much happiness."

She squeezed his hand, "I am happy...happier than I deserve or ever expected!"

When Elias and Nathaniel arrived at Ishi's home, they found friends had already started to gather. Ishi dressed in his very best robe. The arrival of male members of the bride's family was the signal that everything was in readiness. Ishi had started stocking his larder for the feast the day Zipporah had said, "Yes." He had a housekeeper, but had hired villagers to help with the preparation of food and to serve it.

Ishi led the wedding guests to Jacob's house. Jacob answered his knock, "Shalom, Ishi."

"Shalom. May I see my bride?" said Ishi as part of the ceremony. He entered the courtyard.

"Your bride awaits you, yonder," Jacob responded.

Zipporah stood beside Philip. Ishi went to her, lifted the veil, and gave the customary shout of joy at the treasure he had found.

Jacob was pouring wine into two cups, and offered them to Ishi and Zipporah. They linked arms before accepting them, put the cups to their own lips for a sip, traded cups and took another sip. Jacob said, "You are now husband and wife. May you have a long and fruitful life together."

Shouts of joy emerged from all the guests. The wine cups were given back to Jacob. Zipporah placed her hand in the crook of Ishi's arm for the first time. They took off, leading the wedding procession through the streets back to Ishi's house. Elias and Nathaniel picked up Philip on his bed, and took him to the wedding feast. Everyone from the house joined in the parade.

Customarily, the act of consummating the marriage was performed in private as soon as the wedding party arrived at the bridegroom's house, while guests waited. The bride and groom went to Ishi's bedroom. He pulled Zipporah to him. She tilted her face so his lips found hers. The thrill of a passionate kiss went through both like a bolt of lightning. Ishi pulled away, then kissed her again lightly, embraced her, holding her close to his chest. "I can hardly wait, Zipporah, but I am going to. I want plenty of time for us both to enjoy ourselves. Is that all right with you?"

Zipporah was relieved to learn already that she and Ishi were thinking alike. She said, "Yes, Ishi, it is perfectly all right. Thank you for your consideration."

They returned to the wedding celebration, hosted the feast with much wine. Men ate together at one table, women and children at another table. As musicians played, the men stood, formed a circle, and placed their hands on the back or shoulder of those next to them. and danced. Then the women danced. Ishi's courtyard was not big enough for all of them to dance at the same time. Men and women did not usually dance together.

Wedding parties of the well-to-do lasted for days, but one-day feasts were more the custom in the village of Bethsaida. These were working people, and everyone had duties early the next morning. Children usually were bedded early. So, shortly after sunset all the guests had departed. When the hired help finished putting everything in order, they were paid and dismissed. Last to go was the housekeeper.

As they turned from bidding her good night, Ishi shyly took Zipporah's hand and said, "Finally! I have you to myself. This does not seem real." He hesitated. When Zipporah said nothing, he continued, "Long ago I dreamed of you being my wife. I must prick myself with a knife to see if I am awake or dreaming again."

"I had no idea that you felt that way, Ishi."

"You were pledged to Mica. He was my friend. I surrendered any thought of you that I had…you know the commandment about not coveting your neighbor's wife. No one knew."

## Chapter Twenty-five

Click! John awoke with a start. Squeaking of hinges indicated the outside door was being opened. The glow of a lighted torch preceded the approach of men. *What is this all about?* John recognized them. They were the soldiers that had arrested him. His heart started to thump in his chest. He arose to a sitting position.

"Come, John. Get to your feet!"

"Am I going to get my hearing ... in the middle of the night? Before all the guests?"

"No! A part of you will be presented to Antipas, before all the guests. But you will not get your hearing," said one guard as another unlocked the cell and tied John's wrists together.

"What do you mean, 'A part of me'?" John asked. He was pulled toward the door of his cell.

"Your head will be presented on a platter." The guard stood eye to eye with John as he said this.

John felt his knees grow weak and discomfort in his stomach. He remembered having said to Hasshub just a few hours earlier that he was ready for whatever Jehovah had for him. Well, if this is what he must do, he would do it for the glory of God! He would not faint. He would be strong.

"That does not sound like Antipas. Whose idea was it?"

"You are right!" They were dragging him up the stairs. "It was Herodias' idea."

"How did Antipas allow his mistress to make such a decision?"

"He made a promise that he couldn't get out of."

"Great! He makes promises, and it costs me my life! I don't understand."

By now the execution party was trudging across the courtyard toward the slaughter pen.

The other guard said, "He had too much wine. He wanted Salome to dance for him. She didn't want to, so he promised her anything she desired if she would dance."

"So, it was Salome who passed sentence!"

"No, not really. She asked her mother what she should say. It is Herodias, all right, who wants your head."

"My mission in life is over, anyway. Did you know that the Messiah has come?"

"How do you know? You have been in prison!"

"I know! And he will turn your world upside down."

Now they reached the yard where animals were slaughtered for food. The yard was ringed with soldiers and kitchen help.

A guard shouts, "Butcher! Get your biggest, sharpest axe. We have a job to do!" John is made to lie face down on the ground with his neck over a plank.

John said, "Make it quick...do a good job," and started chanting a psalm of praise. He didn't get far into the song. It was quick. It was clean.

Hasshub was among the spectators. With the swing of the axe that severed John's head, he became ill. He left the crowd and vomited. He heard one of the soldiers order, "Carry the body outside the wall and give it to his friends." He was one of those the order was meant for, so he woodenly moved back into place. He and another who was in John's class were openly weeping. One of them picked up the arms, the other the legs, and carried it to the gate.

Outside the gate, the disciples had been sleeping. With the opening of the gate, Phinehas and Segub stood to see what was happening. First, a torchbearer came through the opening, and then two soldiers carrying a dead body followed. They came toward their camp. Phinehas called, "Hail! What are you bringing us?"

Hasshub replied, "What is left of John's body."

By now, they were close enough for the men to see that this body had no head. A sense of anger flared through them, along with an emotion of grief. "No! How did this come about?"

"Let me get a cloth for you to lay it on," Segub shouted, as he went toward a supply wagon."

As they waited, Hasshub related the events of the evening. He ended by saying, "We will be bringing you his head, too, as soon as Herodias has her fill of seeing it." The guards seemed reluctant to return to the fortress, but after hesitating as though they wished they could join the group, they turned and went back inside the walls.

Awakened by the commotion, others in the camp came to where Phinehas and Segub were standing.

Everyone was starting to talk at once, asking, "What happened?" and, "Who could commit such a foul act?"

Phinehas in a loud voice said, "Friends!" The crowd quieted with sobs being heard among the women. He continued, "We must remember that John told us his life's work was complete."

Segub added, "Scripture foretold of Elijah coming to prepare the people for the Messiah. ...I think...John...was Elijah!"

The small group of men gasped in awe. They remembered the visits they had with John in the prison, and had not given a thought that he might be Elijah, God's prophet who left the world without dying.

Phinehas speaks, "Now, tonight, we have been bestowed with a great honor and privilege...the body...the remains of a man who was truly a prophet of God."

While they were waiting for the guards to bring them the head, Phinehas asked Segub, "Shall we dig a grave up here or should we put it in our wagon and take it back to the river?"

"John's ministry was by the river. I think he would prefer that. We can find a cave to put the body in and cover the hole with a boulder."

"We need to break camp right now, then, to get this body buried before the next setting of the sun."

Not more than an hour later the soldiers returned with the head, carrying it in a sack. The disciples were ready to leave. The first light of day found the disciples' camp completely deserted.

# Chapter Twenty-six

"We nearly capsized last night from a bad storm," Nathaniel had said one afternoon after arising, while waiting for the evening meal to be readied.

Philip had been lying down, too, but he sat up when Nathaniel came down the stairs. "Tell me about it."

"We were fishing near the mouth of the Valley of the Doves. Maybe you remember...it isn't too unusual for it to be windy in that area."

Philip nodded.

"Well, last night the wind from the west became so strong! Water was washing into the boat...I thought we were going under. Then...all of sudden it was calm. It was eerie! All the fishermen were talking about it this morning as we were unloading. Someone said that Y'shua had done it."

Philip sat up straighter, looked at him sharply and said, "What do you mean, 'had done it'?"

"He calmed the storm," said Nathaniel, throwing both hands in the air.

Philip frowned at him. "What? He did what? What are you talking about?"

"All I know is what I was told." Nathaniel was shaking both hands in front of him. "He was asleep in Simon's boat. I don't know who or how many were with him. They were going to bring in a catch, and this terrible wind came up. They were in danger of being swamped, so they awakened Y'shua to prepare him for what they might have to do."

When he hesitated, Philip said, "Well? Go on!"

"He said to the wind, 'Peace, be still,'…and… it obeyed!"

Philip pulled his body back and said, "Really? That's hard to believe." He rubbed his chin, tilted his head back slightly and stroked his beard with the back of his forefinger and middle finger of his right hand. Then he asked, "Is there more?"

"He calmed the wind! Have you ever heard of such a thing?"

"No! Never! That is the most amazing thing I've ever heard. I wonder… How did he do it?"

"I am told that he stood up, raised his hands…" Nathaniel raised his own hands above his head, "…looked into the wind, and commanded, 'Peace! Be still!'… and it calmed immediately."

The two brothers sat speechless, staring at each other. Finally Philip almost whispered, "What do you make of it?"

Nathaniel, shaking his head, softly answered, "I don't know, Philip." He was silent for a moment. "I just don't know." Commenting more to himself than if he expected an answer, "What kind of power does he have to do this? What manner of man is he?"

These news announcements were the usual way Philip was able to keep up with events.

Another afternoon Nathaniel said, "Your friend, Y'shua, went through Bethsaida yesterday. He is drawing quite a following."

"Oh," Philip groaned. "I wish I had known…I would liked to have seen him. Do you know yet what he is preaching?"

"'Repentance, and the kingdom of God is at hand,' is what I've been told."

"That's what John was preaching. I wonder if…Y'shua is his disciple." He hesitated, giving thought to that possibility, then asked, "What else have you heard?"

"Do you remember Ithiel, the blind man here in Bethsaida?"

Philip said eagerly, "Yes. What about him?"

"I was told he was brought to Y'shua for healing."

Philip gasped and asked, "What happened?"

"He took Ithiel by the hand and led him out of the village. He then spit on Ithiel's eyes…"

"…Spit?… On his eyes?"

"That's what I was told. And then he laid his hands upon him and asked him, 'Do you see anything?'"

"Could he?" Philip studied Nathaniel's every move and expression.

"He answered, 'I see people, but they look like trees walking.' So Y'shua put his hands on Ithiel's eyes, and his sight was restored…he could see everything clearly."

After waiting for Nathaniel to say more, Philip commented, "Y'shua must be a prophet of God, to be able to calm the wind and restore sight to the blind."

"People are bringing all kinds of sick and disabled persons for him to heal, I am told."

Philip's back straightened. He attempted to mask his intense interest as he asked, "Oh? Such as?"

"Well, such as demoniacs, epileptics, even paralytics..."

"...Paralytics, too?" Philip interjected.

"That's the word going around."

After giving this a bit of thought, Philip said, "The next time he is on this side of The Sea, I would surely like to have you take me to him."

"All right, Philip. If I learn of his coming, I will see that you are carried to him. Usually, by the time I hear, he has come and gone."

"Yes, I know...you work all night and rest all day. But I pray that it will come to pass."

Despite the brief happiness Philip enjoyed at Zipporah's marriage, depression was always very close. He had to force himself to perform his teaching chore. Yes, it had become that, a chore. It used to be something he loved: watching the young minds absorb learning as a sponge absorbs water. His night dreams were still beyond his control, and he didn't sleep soundly. The only thing of real interest to him was that which he was periodically hearing of Y'shua. He looked forward to Nathaniel's visit each afternoon—he was the source of the stories.

Then came the dreadful morning when Nathaniel brought the news that John, the Baptist, was dead. Philip's response was immediate, "No! —How do you know?"

"John's disciples brought the details to Y'shua. I learned of it through Zebedee's crewmen."

"How did he die?"

"Beheaded!" Nathaniel exclaimed, watching Philip closely to see how he was going to take the news.

Philip's mouth dropped open. The words were like knives into Philip's heart. He stared vacantly into space, completely stunned. Feeling sick all over, he thought: *what kind of insanity are we living with?* His right hand went to his stomach, the left hand to his mouth, trying to ward off convulsive shakes. The left hand fingers went to his forehead, tears filling his eyes. He turned his hand around and pressed the palm hard against his nose, moving it slowly to cover his mouth. Turning his face heavenward, he started to cry.

Nathaniel dropped to his knees alongside his dear brother, throwing his strong arms around him, gently holding him to his chest.

"I just don't understand, Nathaniel. John was such a dedicated man. He knew exactly what he was doing—helping people; never hurting anyone. What a horrible way to die. And, what a cowardly thing to do. I'm shocked and disappointed in Antipas...I thought he was more tolerant than that!"

Nathaniel released his arms from around Philip, and repeated the story as he had heard it about the celebration; how Antipas was tricked. "It was Herodias, Salome's mother, that told her to ask for John's head."

"She, no doubt, was getting back for him calling her an adulteress."

"Exactly. At least that's the way everyone sees it."

"It's a horrible way to die. Horrible. Absolutely sickening. John was just a holy man preaching at the Jordan."

Philip had no appetite for food at the evening meal. Even though he was tired from emotional exhaustion, sleep didn't come to him that night. He hadn't slept soundly for two years, but seldom did he wrestle the whole night without dozing a little.

Reviewing his entire experience with John, beginning with the first day at Qumran, he questioned his own worth, thinking: *I'm a bad omen to those with whom I come in contact: Hannah, Mica, and now John. Who will be next? My father? mother? one of my children? I am a burden—first to the kind people at Qumran and now to my family—by having to be carried everywhere, and waited on. Why can't I just die and leave this miserable world behind?*

With the dawning of a new day, he thought *I cannot face life's challenges any more—I want to end it all.* Without moving from his lying position, he said to his mother, "Tell the boys I am ill. Send them to the synagogue until I can take them again."

She replied, "Where do you feel sick, Philip? I can fix something to make you better."

"I can't eat anything. My pain is all over. Just leave me alone."

With a worried look, she turned away. As the students arrived, she sent them to the synagogue.

Philip turned on his side with his back to the courtyard, and pulled his bed robe up over his eyes to shield them from the light. Fitful sleep eventually came.

When Jacob and Elias came from the synagogue, they tried talking to Philip, but he was uncommunicative. He wanted them to go about their duties, and forget him.

The same thing happened when Nathaniel came downstairs from his day's rest—the time Philip usually heard whatever news Nathaniel had to give him about Y'shua.

He declined offers of food, "I have no appetite."

The little girls had established a habit of sitting with their father after the evening meal, just before going to bed. He made an effort to respond to their persistent chatter. He forced a smile and kissed each one. "Good night, little ones," he said as they left to go upstairs.

The next day was a repeat of the day before. By the third day, Philip was noticeably weaker. His loved ones were becoming frantic to do something to bring him out of his depression. But no one could even talk to him, except his daughters. He continued to make an effort to give them his attention.

## Chapter Twenty-seven

"Abba, Prisca and I had the same dream about you last night," Phoebe said one evening, before his severe depression, when Philip was having private time with his girls,

Prisca chimed in, "You were walking, just like you used to."

Ruth added, "That was my dream!"

Philip had become accustomed to Phoebe and Prisca's dreams of prophecy, but this was the first he knew of Ruth also having the gift. The girls' dreamed about their friends and members of the family, and what they foresaw usually came true within a week or two. Sometimes their dreams were beyond the mundane. Philip resisted the reasonable attitude to discard them as fantasy, and kept them in his memory for future reference. This was not the first time they had seen him walking.

Philip looked from one to the other's upturned faces, deep into their dark, serious eyes. Their positive attitude reminded him of their mother, Hannah. Oh! How he missed her—every day. His heart wanted to yield to the imploring look of his little girls and agree with them, but his practical sense told him, *"No! They are just the wishful dreams of children."*

He kissed each one, and said, "Thank you for sharing your dreams. Good night, dear ones." The other family members were waiting for Jacob to say the evening prayer so they could go upstairs with them and to their own beds.

Philip was so tired. *I know I am starving myself. I long to believe in my daughters' dreams, but I am still paralyzed and a burden. I welcome death. It saddens me to think of missing out on the growth and marriage of my children. But with them being named heirs of Ishi and Zipporah, the inheritance would insure good marriages. I am so grateful for that.* His final thought was a deep yearning to see Y'shua again.

He fell into a deep sleep. He rested as he had not since before his wife's death. After several hours of 'slumber he dreamed, not of Hannah as usual, but of himself, on his pallet in the courtyard.

He seemed to be floating upward, out of his body. He could see it lying on the bed. *How thin it is! Oh! What a relief to be free of that burden!*

Upward he drifted. Now visible was the whole village of Bethsaida nestled between hills and sea. Lights on the boats showed where the fishermen were at work. *I wonder if I can find Nathaniel,* and instantly he was over Nathaniel's boat. One of the crew was on watch, Nathaniel and the other crewman were letting out the net.

Try as he could, Philip was unable to get Nathaniel's attention. Philip continued on his upward flight. He was high enough now to see the entire Sea of Galilee below him as a small lake, surrounded by hills on the east and west, higher hills and mountains on the north—*there is snow-capped Mount Hermon— and the Jordan Valley to the south. What a thrill to view your home ground from this elevation!*

A brilliant light was blotting out the scene below. Such joy, serenity, and love! These emotions had never been so intense. Within the light, a shape began to emerge. It is a person? —it is Y'shua! The kindest voice he ever heard said, "You must go back, Philip. It is not yet your time."

"No! I want to leave that body in the courtyard, and stay here with you."

"You have a mission to fulfill. Your body will be healed at the proper time."

Reluctantly, Philip submitted his desire to Y'shua's command to return to his body. Instantly he was in the courtyard, on his bed. The jolt of returning awakened him still sensing the frustration of having to come back.

What a fabulous dream! It was so vivid! As he reviewed it, he thought: *surely it must have great meaning. I need that encouragement so badly. Was it more than just a dream? No one will believe that I died and talked to the spirit of Y'shua and he sent me back.* "You have a mission to fulfill," he had said. Not only that but, "Your body will be healed at the proper time."

## Chapter Twenty-eight

Dawn was beginning to break. The family will be coming down soon. I can hardly wait to ask Mother for something to eat. I am starved!

He was sitting up on his pallet as his mother, the first to come down stairs, looked at him, wide-eyed. "God be with you, Mother," he cheerfully greeted her.

She hurried to his bed, "And also with you, my son. How good it is to see you awake!" she said and bent to kiss the top of his head.

"I am much better, and hungry! Do you have something to feed a starving man?"

"Oh, yes, I have plenty, but you will not be able to eat but very little. You haven't eaten for three days…I'll bring you some nourishment." She left to fix a plate of eggs and bread.

As the other members came down the stairs, they were similarly greeted, and Philip was welcomed back to the land of the living by one and all.

Philip relished the food, and his mother was right. Two eggs and a piece of bread was all he wanted. However, after about two hours, he felt hungry again. She very happily fixed him another plate.

Philip looked forward to Nathaniel's return from his boat. He usually came home by the third hour after sunrise, at the latest. Four hours passed, and still no

Nathaniel. Because of his dream, Philip was positive he had not been in a storm at sea.

He didn't want to alarm Elizabeth, but at the fifth hour he asked her, "Was Nathaniel going somewhere today?"

"No, Philip," she replied, "I'm concerned that he hasn't come home or sent a message."

"Well, he's probably all right, and will have a good story to tell us when he does come."

# Chapter Twenty-nine

"Father Jacob! Nathaniel has not come home! I am so worried," Elizabeth said greeting Jacob and Elias at about the sixth hour as they entered the courtyard from the synagogue.

Their spirits had been high all morning because of Philip's sudden turn-around, but they plummeted with this news. Every fisherman's family has a constant, nagging, concern for the safety of their loved ones while they're at sea.

Jacob, putting his arms around his daughter-in-law, said, "Don't fret, dear one. We will go to the market place and learn what we can." As she pulled away, he added, "Try not to worry...it's not good for the little one you are carrying."

"Thank you, Father Jacob, but...I am deeply concerned."

Jacob and Elias hurried to the waterfront where Nathaniel tied his boat. It wasn't there. No one had news of an accident. They learned the sea had been calm all night, which helped to relieve their worry of a sinking.

The crewmen of the other boats were home sleeping. Perhaps Zebedee, who had a hired crew, would know. So they went to the home of Zebedee and Salome, his wife.

The house was one of the largest in Bethsaida, evidence of the business success enjoyed by Zebedee.

Jacob and Elias knocked on the courtyard door, which was answered by a servant. She recognized them and invited them into the courtyard.

"Shalom. We have come to speak to Zebedee," Jacob said.

"I'm sorry. He's not here."

"May we speak to Salome then?" Elias asked.

"No, she isn't here, either. I'm sorry," she answered.

"Can you tell me where I can find them? Nathaniel didn't come home this morning, and we hoped Zebedee would have some information," Jacob said.

"They are in Capernaum. The new rabbi has been teaching on the hillside near there for two or three days. They are there."

Capernaum was across the sea from Bethsaida, on the western shore.

Elias said, "We heard their sons, James and John, were disciples of the new rabbi, but we didn't know that Zebedee and Salome were too."

She said, "Zebedee has to tend to his businesses, so he does not follow him everywhere, but Salome tries to. Y'shua's mother is her sister."

Jacob and Elias looked at each other at this revelation.

The maid continued, "We help with provisions from our store room. My master says, 'The more I give, the more my businesses grows.' It takes much to feed everyone."

A little surprised, Jacob asked, "How many people are there?"

"The rabbi has selected twelve men for his inner circle of companions. He has given them the power to heal as he does, and is preparing them to go out in pairs to teach and preach and heal."

"What will they be preaching, do you know?" Jacob asked.

"Repent, for the kingdom of heaven is at hand."

Elias asked, "Isn't that what John the baptizer was preaching?"

"Yes," she answered. "I went with my master and mistress many times to hear John down on the Jordan. I also like to listen to Y'shua, but I had to stay here today, and allow someone else to go."

Elias, inspired, asked his father, "Do you think Nathaniel may have stayed in Capernaum to listen to the rabbi?"

His worried face brightening, Jacob said, "He may have. Philip is very interested in hearing everything he can about him."

Turning to the servant, Jacob said, "Thank you so very much. Give our greetings to Zebedee and Salome."

That, indeed, was what Nathaniel and his crew of two had done. It was the day of preparation—Sabbath began with the setting of the sun—and they could rest that night in their beds. So, after marketing their catch in Capernaum, they left their boat tied at the waterfront, and went in search of the rabbi. Querying the fish dealer as to which direction to take, they went into the hills behind Capernaum.

Soon they overtook others who were also looking for the teacher. After climbing the mountain that showed much trampling, they reached a hillside that was peopled with listeners seated on the ground.

Nathaniel guessed they numbered in the thousands. Men outnumbered the women and children, but there were many of them, too. He didn't know that many people lived in the area surrounding the Sea of Galilee. He later learned they had come from far away places, too, such as Jerusalem to the south, and Tyre and Sidon to the west on the coast of the great sea.

Farther on up the hill, seated on a large boulder outcropping, was the speaker. Although he was not shouting, his voice was carrying very well to where they were. Nathaniel and his companions quietly sat down near the people at the edge of the crowd. Soon others joined them, and it wasn't long until more listeners surrounded them. The crowd continued to grow each hour of the day.

The rabbi seemed to be strengthening the Law. He said, "One of the commandments is 'You shall not commit adultery.' I say if you even look at a woman with lust, you have already committed adultery with her in your heart. If your eye causes you to sin, pull it out and throw it away. If your hand causes you to transgress, chop it off. It is better you lose a part than that your whole body go to the rubbish heap."

Nathaniel was mulling over this enlargement of the commandment when the teacher said, "Another commandment is 'You shall not kill' and added to it is 'Whoever kills shall be liable to judgment.' I say whoever is angry with his brother shall be liable to judgment; if you insult your brother, you are liable to the council, and if you say, 'You fool!' you are liable to the fire of the rubbish heap."

He continued, "Along those lines, you have heard it said, 'An eye for an eye and a tooth for a tooth.' I say do not resist those who wish to do evil to you. If you are struck on the right cheek, turn so he can strike the other one. And if he wants your coat, give him your cloak, too. If you are asked to go a mile, go the second mile as well. Give to those who beg and refuse not those who wish to borrow."

He was going too fast—Nathaniel felt he needed time to think about these additions to the laws that were so much a part of his upbringing. The rabbi seemed to be speaking with authority—as though he was absolutely certain that what he was stating would be accepted. The common expression of "The Lord thus said" was absent—he was using "I say…"

Y'shua continued, "And when you give, keep it a secret. Do not be like the hypocrites in the synagogues and on the streets that make sure their generosity is seen. When you give, do not let your left hand know what your right hand is doing."

Now that is something to consider. I will never be able to remember all of this to tell Philip.

After a slight pause, the rabbi said, "Be cautious about who is near when you do good deeds. If you are rewarded by the attention of men, you will have lost your reward from your Father who is in heaven."

And so it went all day: Y'shua speaking of a new way of daily living and Nathaniel wishing he had more time to dwell on each thought.

He suddenly realized how long it would take to go home. They had walked about an hour to come to this place, and the crossing would take another two hours. He was shocked to see how low in the sky the sun was. He whispered to his crewmen, "We don't have time to get home before the Sabbath begins. We will have to stay here overnight and tomorrow, too."

One answered, "I hope the message to our families was delivered! And I did not bring anything to eat."

The other said, "Neither did I."

Nathaniel said, "That makes three of us! We will just have to fast." Then he became aware of Y'shua conferring with Simon and Andrew and other disciples who were nearest to him.

The people were starting to get restless; some stood up. Y'shua said to the crowd, "Sit on the grass. You will be fed." Nathaniel and his crew looked at each other and smiled. By this time there must be 5,000 men, not counting the women and children. *How could he feed this multitude? It would take many wagons full of food. Where were they?*

In one hand Y'shua held up two smoked fish and in the other, a sack with bread. Y'shua looked up, said a blessing, took one loaf and broke it.

Philip experienced the feeling he often did during a lightning storm—a peculiar charge in the air.

Y'shua gave the loaves and fish to his many helpers. When they turned around, each had a basket full of fish and bread! They in turn gave them to the people.

It took a long time—about half an hour—for one to come by where Nathaniel and his crew were seated. He did not recognize him. The man said, "Take the amount you need." Philip took some bread and a piece of fish, amazed that it had lasted this far back into the crowd. And plenty remained!

After everyone had eaten as much as they wanted, the disciples went among the people and gathered twelve baskets of broken pieces! *How can I convince anyone that this really has happened?*

As the sun set, the Sabbath was beginning. James and John stood and led the crowd in psalm singing, and then Y'shua started teaching again. After about an hour, another psalm was sung, a prayer said, and everyone was released for the night. It was still light enough for Nathaniel to look for Zebedee and Salome. Finding them, and after exchanging greetings, it was from them he learned more about the happenings for the past day or two, and where the people came from.

Nathaniel said, "I can not believe what I saw just now...where did the food come from? I see no wagons with provisions."

"It is another of Y'shua's miracles. He had nothing but two fish and five loaves. With his blessing, they multiplied to more than was needed."

"You said, 'Another,' what others has he done? He heals, I have heard of that. Are there others?"

"Oh, yes! The first one that I heard about was at a wedding in Cana. The bridegroom ran out of wine. Y'shua had the servants fill the casks with water, but when it was poured, it was excellent wine. The guests were unaware of what had happened...they thought the bridegroom had saved his best for last. But we and the servants knew."

"He is surely blessed by God," Nathaniel replied.

Zebedee said, "You should bring Philip to the Master, Nathaniel. He will heal him."

Nathaniel answered, "He is sick now, but when...or if...he recovers, we will try to get him out the next time Y'shua comes to our side of the sea.

Will you let me know ahead of time so I can arrange to have my crew help?"

Zebedee nodded and said, "Has Philip yet heard about the death of John the Baptist?"

"Yes. That news is the cause of his illness. He has not recovered from the shock. I am fearful that he is going to die."

"No! Encourage him to get well enough to come to the Master. He will make him well."

"How long have you been up here?"

"Y'shua came yesterday. Salome and I think he wanted to get away by himself after receiving the sad news about John, but the people followed him. He is such a considerate, compassionate man that he let them stay. He has been teaching now for two days. Tomorrow will be the third."

"From what I have heard, he is expanding the concept we have of our way of life."

"Yes. He started out with a list of blessings for eight or ten different kinds of people...what their rewards will be."

Nathaniel said, "I don't understand."

"Well, for instance, he said, 'Blessed are the pure in heart, for they shall see God,' mourners will be comforted, the meek will inherit the earth, and several others."

"Oh...more food for thought."

"John and James will have all of them word for word. When you get a chance to talk to them, they can tell you. Y'shua is training his twelve disciples to go out in pairs of two and do that which he does."

"How do they feel about it?" Nathaniel asked.

"They are getting excited, and somewhat anxious. Some people are opposed to what Y'shua is doing and preaching. The Pharisees and Sadducees are starting to follow him around to try to trip him. My sons know that they will be facing the same kind of behavior."

"Well, they have more courage than I do. My wish is God's peace for them." After chatting a few minutes longer, Nathaniel said, "Now I'd better go back to my friends. We did not expect to stay over the Sabbath. I hope our families received the messages we sent."

"Good night, Nathaniel," Zebedee and Salome said together.

Nathaniel and his crew were accustomed to the night air at sea. When working the nets, robes were cumbersome, so they usually stripped to their loincloths. This night they were fully clothed and, though the mountain air was colder than they were used to, they had no trouble sleeping warmly.

The morning dawned into a beautifully clear day. A year-round natural spring higher up the mountain had made a little stream nearby from which drinking water was obtained.

James and John started the Sabbath Day service. They once again led the multitude in psalm singing.

Then Y'shua stood and from memory quoted the prophet Isaiah: "Cry aloud, lift up your voice like a horn; tell my people of their transgressions, to the house of Jacob their sins."

In a softer voice, he continued, "Yet they look for me everyday, and delight to learn my ways, as if they were a people that did the right things and did not forget the ordinance of their God; they ask of me correct judgment, they are happy to come near to God."

Speaking with inflections God may have used, he kept on quoting scripture, "They say, 'Why have we fasted and you didn't see it? Why have we put ourselves down, and you didn't acknowledge it?' I say, 'The day of your fast you look for your own pleasure and oppress all your employees. You fast only to quarrel and to fight and to hit with wicked fist.'"

Then Y'shua seated himself on the boulder and started preaching about fasting, saying, "When you fast, do not look unhappy, like the hypocrites. They scowl that their fasting may be observed by men." Knowing looks were exchanged among the people in the crowd. "I say, that is their reward. When you fast, anoint your head and wash you face as you usually do, that no man will know. Your Father, who knows your secret, will reward you."

And that was just the beginning of a day full of such life-enriching pearls. He talked about treasures—store them in heaven; not judging people—you may likewise be judged; not to be anxious about life—God takes care of the birds, and people are more important than birds; and those who hear his words and act on them are like men who build their houses on rocks rather than on sand.

Then he turned to how to pray, saying, "Do not be obvious, but go into a secret place and pray to your Father, who knows your secrets and will reward you."

One of the disciples said, "We do not know how to pray."

He said, "I will teach you, and we will close with you repeating the prayer. This is how you should pray: Our Father in heaven, holy is your name."

At the words "Our Father" a gasp came from the audience, and a buzz of whispering. No one had ever called the great Jehovah "Father"!

Raising his voice he said, "Now, everyone, repeat after me: Our Father... "The combined voices of the multitude sounded like an ocean roar as the people said together each line, after he had said it. "Your kingdom come, your will be done on earth as it is in heaven. Give us today our daily bread. Forgive us our debts and transgressions, as we forgive our debtors and those who transgress against us. Lead us away from temptations, and deliver us from evil." The sun was setting as last tones faded away. The Sabbath was over.

Nathaniel said, "We must get back to the boat. We can sleep in shifts until the net is full." But to himself he said, *I can hardly wait to tell Philip all that I've seen and heard.*

# Chapter Thirty

"Wake up, Nathaniel!" a crewman whispered loudly. "I am seeing something on the water that I can't make out."

"What do you see?" Nathaniel asked softly, suddenly wide-awake, coming to his feet and looking in the direction the other man was staring.

"It looks like a ghost. And it's going toward Simon's boat."

It was about two hours before dawn, and the moon had set. The sky was clear. Reflection of starlight was the only natural light. Each boat had an oil lamp to attract the fish. The westerly wind had driven the boats far from shore. Most of the boats were owner-operated, and each went where the fishing was good. Consequently, they would gather in the same area, within hailing distance of each other.

As Nathaniel looked, he, too, saw a softly lighted cloud moving over the water toward Simon's boat. Just then he heard cries of fear coming from that vessel. He heard, "It's a ghost!" Then from the cloud came, "Be not afraid. It is I." Nathaniel recognized the voice of Y'shua and immediately he could see that it was indeed him—walking—on the sea!

Astonishment filled Nathaniel's being. He turned to look at his crewman, and saw a reflection of his own incredulous expression.

He heard Simon's voice say, "Master, if it is you, let me come to you." Nathaniel knew that Simon was impulsive, but surely he knew that he could not walk on water!

Y'shua answered, "Come." *Will Simon actually try it?* He didn't have long to wait. As he watched, Simon climbed out of his boat and walked toward Y'shua! "Are you seeing what I think I am?" he asked his crewman.

"If you are seeing Simon walking on the sea, then I am!" came his reply.

Nathaniel said, "It is hard enough to accept that Y'shua can, but to see Simon do it is really beyond belief!"

Just then, Simon started to sink and cried, "Save me!"

Y'shua reached out and caught him by the hand. As they jumped into the boat, Y'shua asked, "What caused you to lose faith?"

Nathaniel and his crewman strained to hear Simon's response, but all they could make out was the word "wind". It had been gusting, but it stopped and became calm as soon as Y'shua and Simon boarded the boat. Nathaniel said, "I can not believe what I just saw! Can you?"

His friend answered, "He surely has unusual powers...to calm the storm, feed that multitude yesterday with so little food, and now this!"

"It makes me wonder, what next?" He hesitated, "Surely, Y'shua must be a prophet."

Among the crowd going back from the mountain to Capernaum earlier that evening were the fishermen-disciples with whom Nathaniel was acquainted. They told him that Y'shua had called James and John "Sons of Thunder." Zebedee had a hearing impairment for many years and habitually shouted when he talked. Y'shua had healed him, so he no longer was "thunder." They told him of many of their experiences as followers of Y'shua. From them he learned the details of John's death, as they walked along the path toward their boats. Nathaniel said, "What an appalling event!"

They told Nathaniel that Y'shua was making his headquarters at the home of Simon's mother-in-law in Capernaum, but that he had stayed behind in the mountain this night to be by himself. "John's death has some kind of special meaning to him," Simon said.

"He seems to be taking it rather hard." John said, "His preaching has changed. Did you notice?"

His brother James said, "Yes, I did. Always before he preached more or less the same message that John was preaching."

John added, addressing Nathaniel, "We twelve disciples are going out soon, and we will be giving the same message about the kingdom of God being at hand."

"What does that mean, John?"

"Nathaniel, we believe Y'shua is the Messiah…a new David."

Another disciple whom Nathaniel learned was named Judas broke in and said, "He's here to restore God's chosen people to Himself, and to establish a new kingdom,"

"From what I heard up on the mountain, he does not plan any military action. How is he going to do it?" Nathaniel asked.

Judas replied, "He's young yet. Give him time. Did you see the size of the crowd? He's being followed everywhere he goes. It'll not be much longer...soon he will start giving us that training."

John said, "Judas, where did you get that idea? He is not teaching  military strength."

Nathaniel said, "John, do you really believe that he is the Messiah?"

"Yes, Nathaniel, I do. What a thrill for me to know that this is happening during my lifetime...and he has chosen me...to be one of his disciples!"

Walking along beside John, Nathaniel experienced a thrill of his own. "What a time to be alive," he echoed. "Imagine! The long-awaited Messiah right here among us Galileans! I have much to tell Philip."

When the people reached Capernaum, some went to their homes, some found a place to spend the night on the ground, and some went to their boats. Nathaniel and his crew planned to put in a night of fishing, as did the other fishermen.


Later that morning as Nathaniel came through the door into the courtyard, he was hoping Philip would be awake and able to talk to him. Usually Nathaniel would eat the food Elizabeth put out for him and go directly up the stairs to his bed. But this morning he was too full of excitement to try to sleep. He returned home as soon as his boat docked—he wanted to share his joy with Philip.

His hopes were answered. Philip had been anxious about Nathaniel's absence. The message of his going to Capernaum had been delivered to Jacob and Elias at the synagogue the day before. But remnants of anxiety remained.

At the first sound of the latch moving on the door, Philip sat up on his pallet. As Nathaniel came through the door, Philip softly called, "Nathaniel?"

He answered, "Yes, Philip, it's me. I'm glad you're awake. How do you feel?"

Philip cried as he held out his arms, "Oh, Nathaniel, I'm so glad you are home safely!"

Nathaniel knelt beside Philip's bed and they embraced.

Philip continued, "I had a fantastic dream that has encouraged me to eat and gain strength."

Sitting back on his heels, facing him, Nathaniel said, "I want to hear your dream, but I have some very important news for you…I have seen the Messiah!"

Philip inhaled audibly and asked, "Is it Y'shua?"

"Yes."

"Are you sure?"

"I have so many things to tell you…I don't know where to begin."

"How do you know that he is the Anointed One?"

"Everything that I heard and saw convinced me. And I talked to Zebedee's son, John. He believes, too."

Philip was aware that he was more emotional since he became paralyzed, and it didn't take much to affect him. This was one of those times. He wanted to laugh for joy. After hundreds of years of his people waiting, looking for and expecting the Messiah, here he was— in their own midst! But weeping was what came. With a choking voice, he said, "I want to hear everything. How about starting at the beginning? If we don't have time, we can finish after your rest."

So Nathaniel began relating his experiences of two days and two nights. He was interrupted when the family came downstairs. His wife, Elizabeth, ran to him, and they embraced. He greeted his father, brother, mother, and Elias' wife, each with an embrace and a kiss. Jacob led the family in Morning Prayer. He and Elias departed for the synagogue, and the women began their daily preparation of meals and household duties. Nathaniel said to Philip, "I shall finish telling you everything this afternoon."

"All right Nathaniel. I can hardly wait. Rest well," Philip replied.

Nathaniel went to the kitchen where he ate his meal and talked to his wife and the womenfolk before starting for the stairway.

In the afternoon, Philip impatiently waited for Nathaniel to come down to the courtyard to finish telling him of the things he had heard and seen.

When Nathaniel went to sleep, he slept soundly all day, until late afternoon. Finally, when he awakened he went downstairs to talk to Philip. Jacob and Elias were home, seated on the earthen floor near Philip. Philip had told them of Nathaniel's conviction that Y'shua was the long-awaited Messiah. They were doubtful but wanted to hear what Philip had to say.

Nathaniel seated himself between Philip and Elias, and repeated to his father and brother that which he had told Philip earlier and continued his narration until he had told all about Y'shua's sayings. They listened very intently. Nathaniel said, "I wish you could hear him. He does not preach...it is more like teaching, than preaching. And he does it with his own authority! You find yourself believing every word he says."

Jacob said, "Tell us again what he said about the law 'You shall love your neighbor'."

"Well, he said, 'You have heard it said, 'You shall love your neighbor and hate your enemy'...Father, I don't remember anything about hating your enemy in the Torah. Do you know where he heard that?"

Jacob frowned, slowly shook his head and said, "The law tells us to be kind to our enemies."

Philip said, "It is in the writings at Qumran. Several places in the literature spell out what they should love and hate."

Three pairs of astonished eyes were on Philip. Jacob said, "Such as?"

Philip answered, "Such as, 'To love all the sons of light, each according to his lot in the Council of God, and to hate all the sons of darkness, each according to his guilt in the vengeance of God'."

Elias said, "That's not exactly 'hate your enemy'."

Philip answered, "How about 'Eternal hatred with the men of the pit'?"

Elias said, "That is not much different, but since you say Y'shua was there, that is probably where he heard it...'hate your enemy'."

Jacob said, "What did he say about it?"

Nathaniel answered, "He said that we are to love our enemy and pray for those that persecute us. That will make us sons of our Father in heaven, for he causes rain to fall on the just and unjust alike, and the sun to shine on evil ones as well as on good people." He paused and looked at Jacob and then Elias, who were studying his every expression.

He continued, "He asked what reward do we receive if we love only those who love us...he said, 'Even the tax-collectors do that.' If we salute only those in our own neighborhood, what is so special about that? The Gentiles do that. Then he said, 'You must be perfect, as your heavenly Father is perfect.' So he enlarged the law of loving our neighbor to being as perfect as Jehovah, who loves the good and bad, the weak and the strong."

Jacob said thoughtfully, "I can find no argument with that, nor any of the other teachings you have spoken about."

"You haven't heard about the miracles I saw with my own eyes!" Nathaniel said.

Philip quickly said, "Miracles? Tell us."

And then Nathaniel told his listeners about feeding the multitude with just two fish and five loaves of bread. When he had finished, Jacob said, "Could it be that many of the people had fish and bread of their own and added them to the baskets?"

Nathaniel said, "I suppose it is possible, but I saw no one take any food from their own sack."

Philip reminded Nathaniel, "You said miracles. That is one. I want to hear about the others."

Nathaniel exclaimed, "Only one other, but what an exciting one it was! Listen to this." And he related the scene on the water he and his crewman had witnessed during the night.

When he finished, the three men were looking at each other, speechless. The women in the background had stopped their talking when Nathaniel had begun his report. The only sounds in the courtyard were from the animals and the little children.

Nathaniel added, "That is why I believe Y'shua is the Messiah." He paused, when no one else said anything, he continued, "I know that each of you will have to decide for yourself. But I am certain that in time you will agree."

Philip said, "I am inclined to believe...even when I saw him as a stranger in Qumran I sensed something different about the man." His voice breaking with the emotion he was feeling, continued, "Nathaniel has told me that he will take me to him the next time Y'shua is on this side of the sea."

Nathaniel sympathetically replied, "Yes, Philip, I will. Zebedee told me he would try to let me know so I can arrange for my crew to help."

Elias said, "I will help, too, if I am available."

Philip, weeping, said, "I know that he can heal me."

The women signaled that the evening meal was ready. After washing and praying, the family gathered around the table and the discussion continued. Each one asking Nathaniel questions about those things he had seen and heard.

# Chapter Thirty-one

Early in the morning seven days later Nathaniel and one of his crewmen came running to the courtyard door. It burst open, startling Philip, his students, the women, and even the animals in their pen. Everyone's head turned to look at them.

"The rabbi is in Bethsaida! He is teaching from a boat to the crowd on the shore," Nathaniel excitedly reported. "We have come to take you down."

Philip's heart leapt in his chest. *Is it today that I shall be healed,* he asked himself. *What shall I do with the boys? Take them with me—give them an opportunity to see the Messiah. Yes! That's what I'll do.*

"We must take the boys with us," Philip replied. Turning to his students, he said, "You would like to hear the new rabbi, wouldn't you?"

All six boys exuberantly welcomed the change of routine with vocal assents.

Philip said, "I want my daughters to hear him, too." Then he shouted, "Zipporah!" She had continued the established routine by coming to the children in their home.

She came running to the head of the stairway. Startled to be summoned in this manner, sharply asked, "What is it, Philip?" All four girls gathered around her.

"Y'shua is in Bethsaida, and Nathaniel is here to take me to him. Can you bring the girls so they can see him too? The boys are going."

"Yes! Yes! We will be glad to," she replied as they descended the stairs.

Meanwhile, Nathaniel had gone to where Elizabeth, Mary and Sarah were working and said, "I would like for you to hear him, too." Stimulated at the probability of Y'shua being the long-awaited Messiah, and being within their own village caused excitement to fill each person in the courtyard. And the possibility of seeing their beloved son and brother healed of his paralysis made the trip even more desirous.

They looked at each other. First Elizabeth and then the others exclaimed, "I would love to go."

Nathaniel and his crewman picked up Philip lying on his bed, one on each end of the carrying poles around which the skin was wrapped. The lads fell in behind, with the women and girls bringing up the rear. When they were out of the courtyard, the boys came alongside the litter, but the women and girls remained behind it. The weather was clear and calm, but the early morning chill was still in the air.

The distance from the house to where the people were was four or five times as far as from the house to the synagogue. Philip and his carriers could tolerate that shorter distance without stopping to rest. But after they had traveled about halfway to the seashore, Nathaniel said, "Let us stop and catch our breath for just a minute. How are you doing, Philip?"

"I could use more padding on this skin; otherwise, I am all right. You two stop as often as you want...I don't want you to get too tired."

The fish market occupied the center of the business district on the waterfront. Other vendors were on both ends. Then came a number of homes before the seashore was free of structures. A small crowd of people was standing there, at the outer edge of the village. It was growing with new arrivals from the village.

Offshore a short distance was the boat the rabbi was in. The morning sun was on his face. The reflection of it in his light brown hair created a glow around his head. His blue eyes were hidden behind a squint. The rust red color of his robe was made more vivid from the sun's brilliance.

As the litter party approached, they could hear Y'shua's voice. Since everyone was standing, and to make it possible for Philip and the children to see the rabbi, they made their way to the water's edge. Even so, they were far from the boat.

He seemed to be telling a story about a farmer sowing his crop and where the seeds landed. Philip feasted his eyes on the man, thinking: *could he really be the Messiah?* He could make no sense of the story; perhaps if he had heard the first part it would have helped.

Then the teacher gave a series of examples of what the kingdom of heaven is like—a precious pearl that a person would sell everything he owned to possess; leaven in bread; a tiny mustard seed growing into a big tree. Without interpretation or time to give thought to the words Y'shua was saying, Philip could not follow.

Someone from the crowd shouted, "What about John?"

Y'shua said, "So you want to know about John. Believe me when I say that no one greater than John the Baptist was ever born of woman." A murmur from the crowd let him know they agreed. Y'shua continued, "Yet a lowly member of the kingdom of God is greater than he." The crowd protested.

Philip thinks: *he is talking in riddles—I am not understanding anything he says.*

Now Y'shua goes on, "The kingdom of God has suffered violence from the time of John, and the violent ones are struggling to take it. You know the law and the prophets: they prophesied until John. You may believe it or not, but I tell you that he is Elijah, who was to come before the kingdom could arrive."

Philip remembered that when he first met John at Qumran, he thought of Elijah and wondered why. Elijah was the prophet of God who was taken from earth without dying. The prophet Malachi wrote that God will send Elijah before the Messiah arrives. *So that was the role John had to play,* Philip thought. *I wonder if he knew that he was the reincarnation of Elijah—I do not think he did. If John was Elijah, as Y'shua just now said he was—the forerunner of the Anointed One, then Y'shua must be the Christ, the Greek word for "Messiah."*

What else is he saying? "Ears are made to hear with…" He had put his hands to his ears, then as he said, "Use them!" he brought them down twice emphasizing each word. He paused, as though he were trying to find the right words. "How can I show you about yourselves…your generation? You are witnesses to the beginning of the kingdom of God, but you will not take part. You are like children playing games in the marketplace. 'We play at having a wedding, and you will not dance; we play a funeral and you would not cry!' John came with his strict diet and camel skin garment and you said, 'He is crazy!' The Son of Man came, eating and drinking, and you say, 'He is a drunkard and a glutton, a friend of tax-collectors and sinners.'" He looked down, and took a deep breath. Philip had felt himself holding his breath, waiting for his next utterance. As though to himself Y'shua said, "Oh, well, the results will tell whether wisdom stands or falls."

He signaled that he was ready to go. Some of his disciples pulled the anchor aboard and the boat was turned to head out to sea.

Philip felt limp from the disappointment. After all the effort Nathaniel had made to bring him down here! His mother observed his dejected posture, came over and gently put her hand on his shoulder. "Don't give up hope, son. Perhaps he will come again."

The return home was more tiring than the trip to the seashore, because the house was located above the beach on a slight elevation. The women talked among themselves, but the men's conversation was minimal. Within their minds, they were reviewing that which they had heard, and evaluating its worth. How could they tell Jacob and Elias what they had heard, when they didn't know themselves? If they could remember the exact words, perhaps Jacob could make some sense out of them.

They were back in time for the boys to return to their homes at the usual time and Jacob and Elias to come from the synagogue.   Nathaniel and Philip thanked the crewman for his help.

The crewman gave them a slight, friendly bow, and said, "I'm sorry that you couldn't receive a healing this morning, Philip.  If the chance comes again, you can depend on me to help."

"Thank you very much," Philip answered as he grasped the crewman's hand in a gesture of warmth and appreciation for his unselfish help. "I have faith that we will be getting another opportunity."

The crewman nodded and gave Philip a friendly smile and departed. As the family gathered around the table for their first meal of the day, Philip and Nathaniel tried to tell Jacob and Elias that which they had heard.  Inasmuch as they had no understanding, they tried to remember Y'shua's sayings word for word.  The other two men failed to comprehend, too.

Jacob said, "There is probably more hidden under the surface that he wants his listeners to ponder.  Let us pray and think on it, and when we come together this evening, we will talk about it again."

The sons agreed that this was a good plan.  The men went to their afternoon duties.  Jacob and Philip used the family table for their trade.  Elias and his young son went to the field, Nathaniel, to his room for sleep.

After the evening meal, Philip shared an insight he had received as to the meaning of the words heard that morning.  He said, "It has come to me that Y'shua's words, 'Ears are made to hear with…use them,' may be a clue to all of his sayings."

Jacob urged him on.

Philip hesitated, "This may be as hard to explain as...perhaps...the true meaning, but I'll try."

Getting a little impatient, Nathaniel said, "Well?..."

Philip answered, "The way I see it, he was using objects with which we are familiar to acquaint us with unseen realities with which we are not familiar...."

"Parables. I have never liked them," Elias interjected.

"Yes. Parables." Philip continued, "We must hear not only the words he used and apply the meaning as we know it from our own experience, but..."

"But what?" asked Nathaniel.

"We must apply a new meaning...something we have not learned before or, with Y'shua's coming, privileged to be witnesses to a new experience." Philip looked from one face to the other to see if any of them had caught his thinking. Their eyes revealed blank stares, as if their minds were searching for understanding.

Philip continued, "For instance, he said the kingdom of heaven is like a rare pearl that a man would sell all his possessions to buy. That one is not hard to get: we are acquainted with the importance of rare pearls and man's desire to own one. So Y'shua is telling us that the kingdom of heaven is worth so much more that we should want to dispose of all our earthly ties to really become a part of it."

After a moment of silence, Nathaniel said, "But he also said it is like yeast in a batch of bread...it cannot be like a pearl and yeast at the same time, can it?"

Philip looked at Nathaniel and said, "What do we know about yeast?"

173

"It causes bread dough to rise," Nathaniel answered.

"Have you ever been in the courtyard when the women had forgotten to knead it down?"

"No."

"Well, I have. The leavening keeps working even after the dough rises out of the bowl it is in, spills down to the table, and on to the floor. Does that tell us anything about the kingdom of heaven?"

"That once it gets started, it will multiply?" Nathaniel tentatively asked.

Philip, starting to feel the part of a rabbi that he used to enjoy so much, said, "Now, let us look at Y'shua...first look at John the baptizer and his ministry."

Jacob said, "Go on."

"John started preaching at a crossing on the Jordan. His message was 'Repent. The kingdom of God is at hand.'" Philip emphasized the words "at hand." "People came to hear him, many repented of their sins and he baptized them in the river. They went home and told their friends and relatives. They went out to hear him. Soon he had a following of thousands of people from all over the country. Does that sound like leavening in bread dough?"

"But John was killed," Elias interjected.

Momentarily saddened by the thought of John's death, Philip slowly answered, "He suffered a horrible death, but...he had served his purpose. He knew he was not the Messiah. What he did know was that he was the one who goes out ahead of the important person to remove the rocks from the roadway." His countenance brightening and with a teasing glint in his eye, said, "Another parable, Elias." Smiles were on all their faces, as they looked at Elias. A small frown returned to Philip's brow as he continued, "As sad as I was to learn of John's death, I know now that it was his time to go and let Y'shua's ministry take over."

As if he suddenly understood, Nathaniel said, "And Y'shua's yeast is a starter from John. Multitudes are following him now! We are alive at the birth of God's kingdom!"

An enlightened Philip added, "And, like the mustard tree, even though it starts out as a tiny seed, it will grow to cover the whole world!"

Elias asked, "Just what is the 'kingdom of God'?"

Silence was the answer, momentarily. Finally Philip found words, "I believe Y'shua has brought it into the world. It is not made up of square feet of territory with boundaries or borders, as we usually define kingdoms. It has started here in Galilee with Y'shua and will spread like leavened bread."

Elias again, "So if it's not physical, it must be spiritual. How can your Y'shua, if he's the Christ, bring a spiritual kingdom, when the Messiah is to be a new David, and restore Judah as a territorial kingdom?"

After a moment's hesitation, and Philip didn't answer, Nathaniel said, "On the way back from the mountain, when I was talking with John, the son of Zebedee, one of the other disciples...Judas was his name...spoke of those expectations, a military leader."

Jacob said, "Go on."

Nathaniel, never too good at memorizing, picked his words slowly, "I am trying to remember how John put it. It was to the effect that Y'shua is teaching them to love one another. John...Zebedee's son...thinks God's kingdom will be based on love, not military might."

Elias said, "I must study the prophets again to see if I have the baptizer being Elijah."

Between Philip and Nathaniel, Y'shua's statements were repeated: The prophets and law were until John. You may believe me or not, but John was Elijah. Since John, the good news of the kingdom of heaven is being preached. From the days of John the kingdom of God has suffered violence, and men of violence try to take it by force. But not one dot of the law will become void.

Jacob said, "At each Passover feast...as you know...we set a place for Elijah at our table, and send our youngest child to the door to see if he has come, because we have been told that Elijah will usher in the Age of the Messiah. And you say that John the baptizer was Elijah?"

Nathaniel answered, "Y'shua said it."

Philip said, "If we substitute the name 'Elijah' for 'John' in Y'shua's statement, I think it will have more meaning." Sensing that Elias was more doubtful of Y'shua actually being the Messiah than was his father, he said, "Try it, Elias."

"The prophets and law were until 'Elijah.' Yes, I can agree with that. At the very last of Malachi's scroll he writes about Elijah returning before the Lord comes," Elias answered.

"The sentence about John preaching the kingdom of heaven means 'The Age of the Messiah is upon us,'" Philip interpreted. Then he said, "Now, Elias, do you remember the next one?"

Elias, having been trained since a very small boy to memorize scripture was proud of his ability to remember sentences verbatim said, "Of course, 'From the days of 'Elijah' the kingdom of God has suffered violence, and men of violence try to take it by force.' I can surely agree with that statement, too! This country has had nothing but warfare and upheaval…all in the name of Jehovah. Chief Priests being deposed and usurped!"

"It's not only this physical kingdom, Elias," Philip quickly replied. "It is spiritual warfare…. Remember, the kingdom of God is a spiritual kingdom!"

Jacob interjected, "Are you saying there is warfare in heaven…angels fighting each other?"

Philip answered, "Maybe…I am just trying to make sense of Y'shua's statement. Since he said, 'Men of violence,' and 'the kingdom of God has suffered violence,' I interpret that as evil spirits influencing the behavior of man. Therefore, God's kingdom…or his plan for us, his people…has suffered."

After a long pause, everyone deliberating on that which had been said, Nathaniel stated, "As much as I would like to remain here and hear more, I must get to the boat. The crew will be ready to sail."

Jacob said, "Well, we have much to think about. This conversation has been very thought-provoking."

Nathaniel said, "Philip, we'll try again to take you to the rabbi for your healing."

"Oh, thank you, Nathaniel. Today was worth the effort, as far as I am concerned. I'm glad to have seen and heard him again."

Elias said, "I will help, too, the next time."

Philip felt a thrill: Elias' curiosity was being aroused.

## Chapter Thirty-two

"Can we talk, Philip?" Jacob asked one afternoon a few days later, before they started their letter writing.

"Yes, Father." Smiling, Philip continued, "Even though we are together every afternoon, we don't visit much, do we?

Jacob seated himself, facing Philip. "I want to know how you are feeling, health-wise."

Looking away momentarily, a weary expression flitted across his face. He answered, "The paralysis has not progressed above my hips, for which I praise God. I no longer have pain. My breathing is difficult at times...I feel like I am suffocating, and I...tend to be more emotional than I used to be."

Jacob nodded as though he agreed, then asked, "How are you getting along with the little boys?"

"We have come to understand each other. They challenged me at first, but have settled down now...especially since my illness."

"Are you satisfied with Zipporah's teaching of your daughters?"

"Oh, yes! They are progressing nicely. I am so happy that she has continued their lessons."

Jacob paused.

Philip studies his father. *What is really on his mind? Small talk is not like him.* As if in answer, Jacob said, "This Y'shua person going around the countryside making people believe he is the Messiah...it is difficult for me to keep an open mind. I

178

have the feeling that you and Nathaniel are believers. Is that so?"

Philip was not ready to commit himself totally, and he wasn't prepared to defend a position. He hesitated before answering. "Father, ... I am not absolutely certain in my own mind...."

Jacob released a breath of relief.

"...but I am leaning toward it. If you could just hear him yourself, you'd be a better judge."

"Had you heard that the Pharisees...and Sadducees, too...are following him, trying to trick him?" Jacob asked.

"Yes, Nathaniel said one of Y'shua's disciples told him. We know the Pharisees are going to fight against anything to keep things the way they are for them—the Sadducees, too, for that matter. So, we shouldn't let their opinions influence our thinking, Father."

"I am finding it hard to believe...after looking for the Messiah for so many generations, that he is really with us...in my lifetime! ...But this Y'shua is not what I expected the Messiah to be."

"Yes, I know...I often feel the same way. However, when Nathaniel tells me about the miracles and his teaching, and then I see and hear him myself, I sense that he is not an ordinary man."

"Have you learned where he is from? Is he from David's line?"

"He is from Nazareth, the son of a carpenter. But he was born in Bethlehem. His father and mother had gone there to register for a census."

Jacob stared at Philip a moment, looked away, and with ill-defined determination asked, "He is about thirty years old, did I hear?"

Philip nodded.

Jacob continued, "That's how old you are, right?"

Philip nodded again, studying his father's countenance for a clue to his reason for asking.

"For the census that year, each man was to register in the home town of his line. Bethlehem was David's home. So that would make him a descendant from the House of David."

Philip sat up straight. Excitedly he asked, "Father! Do you know what you just said?"

Jacob frowned, "Just because he is descended from David does not necessarily make him the Messiah, does it?"

"No, but it makes it even more likely that he is."

Jacob paused, then slowly said, "I remember something else that happened after that census that I shall never forget."

Philip, sensing something important was about to be revealed, said, "Oh? What is it?"

"We were so glad that you were born here in Bethsaida." Jacob hesitated.

Philip said, "What happened?"

"Old King Herod had been told by some visiting royalty that they had come to see the King of the Jews that had just been born."

"'The King of the Jews that had just been born'? How did they know?"

"They came from the east following a special star that guided them westward, and it had led them to Herod's dwelling. According to their legends it was a sign that a king of the Jews had been born."

"What did Herod do?"

"He had his priests look in the Prophecies as to where the Messiah was to be born. They found it to be Bethlehem, the home of David's line. And he asked the kings to return by way of his palace so he would know for sure, and could go to worship him."

When Jacob paused, Philip asked, "What happened?"

Jacob hesitated a moment, looking away, "The kings never came back...they must have gone home another way." Turning to look at Philip, he continued, "Anyway, that didn't stop Old Herod!"

Philip realized his father was unburdening his heart of a memory he would like to forget. He softly asked, "What did Herod do?"

Jacob almost whispered, "He ordered all male babies in the region of Bethlehem, up to two-years old, be murdered!" Jacob's voice caught as he cried, "Oh the slaughter!" He paused. Reflectively added, "A great sadness was over the whole country."

Philip sat stunned. Finally he said, "I have never heard that story."

Jacob whispered, "I know."

After a moment in thought, Philip said, "It sickens me to know that persecution of the Jews is not any less now than when Moses was a baby." Then, brightening, he added, "What you've just told me makes it even more possible that Y'shua is the Messiah. His parents must have been aware he was special ...royalty visiting them would attract attention...so they may have taken the baby away."

"I often wondered," Jacob said softly.

A new thought excited Philip to say, "You said a star? ...a special star led the kings to Bethlehem?"

Jacob said, "Yes, a special star. Some of Herod's priests told me."

"Did you see it?" Philip asked.

"No. I was not out watching the night sky." He hesitated before adding, "But reports from the shepherds in the hills around Bethlehem indicated some unusual happenings in the region at that time."

Philip eagerly asked, "Such as?"

Jacob seemed reluctant, but said, "They said an... angel..." Philip flinched, but Jacob continued, "Yes, an angel appeared to them announcing the birth of a savior in Bethlehem."

"I am amazed...an angel announcing the birth of a savior!"

"Oh, that's not all. A chorus of angels came and sang praises to God."

Indignant, Philip said, "Father! Why have you never told me this before?"

Jacob said, "I suppose because I...I did not want to get my hopes up about a Messiah actually appearing." He hesitated and continued with a wry smile, "And, too, I thought the shepherds may have been celebrating and had a little too much wine."

Philip smiled with him. He was beginning to feel fatigue from this emotional revelation, but wanted to learn everything his father knew of that time. "Is there more to the story?"

Looking away, he answered, "Yes."

When he didn't say more, Philip coaxed, "Well?"

Still looking into space, he said, "The shepherds went to the village and found a newborn baby... "He looked at Philip, who was studying his every move. "... a boy."

Philip nodded for him to continue, "He was lying in a manger...in a stable...of an inn. Because of the census, the inn was full." Staring at Philip, he asked, "Do you want your Messiah to be born in a stable?"

Philip wasn't ready for that question, so he paused as he studied his father's face, then slowly answered, "Before seeing and hearing Y'shua, I would have said, 'No.'" He hesitated. "But between what Nathaniel has told me and... I have heard myself, this Messiah will not be another David...a military conqueror. He is royalty because he is the Anointed One. And Y'shua is teaching a new lifestyle based on love, not might. His followers are common people, from all levels of income...or no income. Having been born in a stable makes him one of them. I can see God's hand in it."

Jacob answered, "I can not, but I shall try to keep an open mind."

"If you would just go out and listen to him the next time he is on this side of the sea..."

"All right! I'll go!" After a few moments of silence he added, "Well, I suppose we should get to our letter writing."

"I hope we don't have many...my mind wants to dwell on these things you have told me."

Jacob said, "Only two," as he dragged the table to Philip's corner.

## Chapter Thirty-three

"Philip!" Jacob called as he and Elias burst through the courtyard door the next day. "You will find this hard to believe...I am having a difficult time, myself!" They had hurried home from the synagogue as soon as their classes ended. Their faces were flushed from the exertion.

Alarmed, Philip asked, "What is it, Father?"

"Do you remember Tahan, the leper?" Elias asked.

"Yes. He has been keeping himself separate from the villagers by living in the hills. Is that the one? What about him?"

"He has been healed!" Jacob fairly shouted as he dropped to his knees beside Philip's bed, tears coming to his eyes.

Stunned, Philip stared at his father and then at Elias, who had also knelt.

"It's true, Philip. I saw him with my own eyes!" Elias confirmed the report.

Jacob said laughing and crying at the same time, "Never in all my life...had I thought I would be called upon to...to perform the priest's ritual after a leper had been healed!"

Philip asked, "What happened?"

Jacob hesitated due to his emotion, so Elias said, "Tahan came to the synagogue this morning and said, 'The rabbi has healed me...'"

"The rabbi? Y'shua?" Philip interrupted.

"The same," Elias answered.

"Tell me all about it," Philip said while smiling broadly.

Jacob sobbed, "No longer am I doubtful. I am convinced Y'shua is the Messiah!"

Philip felt a thrill pass through his body at Jacob's statement. He reached over and lovingly put his hand on his father's shoulder. For a moment he couldn't trust his own voice, but needing to know the whole story, he said, "Go on," as he removed his hand.

Jacob related, "Tahan said to me, 'He told me to show myself to my priest, so here I am. You can see for yourself that I am healed. I have no sores anywhere!' And I couldn't see any."

"Praise God," Philip almost whispered. "What did you do?"

"Well," Jacob hesitated, somewhat embarrassed he continued, "I had to look in the Scriptures to find what I was supposed to do."

All three chuckled.

Elias interjected, "We found it in the Law...a lengthy procedure including an examination 'out of camp,' bringing two clean birds, one to kill and one to dip in the blood of the dead one..."

"Shaving off all his hair and bathing and examining again in seven days," Jacob added.

Philip asked, "Since we do not believe God wants blood sacrifices, what did you do?"

"Elias and I asked him to remove his clothing, and we examined his body. He had no evidence of ever having leprosy!"

"Then Father told him to go home, wash his garments, shave all his hair, bathe his body and return in seven days."

Jacob, laughing, added, "You never saw a happier man!"

"And your friend, Y'shua, did it just because Tahan asked him to," Elias said.

"Did he say how Y'shua did it?" Philip asked.

Jacob answered, "Tahan said that Y'shua stretched out his hand and touched him, a leper! Imagine...touching a leper! As he did he said, 'Be clean.' That is all he did!'

Elias added, "Tahan said that instantly his sores disappeared, and he felt good health restored. Then Y'shua told him to tell no one, but to show himself to his priest."

Philip said, "He will not need to tell anyone...just to be seen will be evidence enough. The same would be true with paralytics." Then resolutely stated, "If he can heal a leper, he can heal me of my paralysis!"

"I agree," Jacob and Elias said simultaneously. And Elias added, "We will see that you have your opportunity."

Jacob added, "I am convinced that at the right time, you will be healed."

# Chapter Thirty-four

"Zebedee asked me to tell you the rabbi is in our area," a fisherman friend said to Nathaniel and Philip at the synagogue on the next Sabbath, after the service. Jacob and Elias, who were nearby and overheard, immediately turned and gave their attention to the speaker.

"Oh? Do you know where?" Nathaniel asked.

"In the hills somewhere behind our village."

"How long will he be there, do you know?" Philip asked.

"Zebedee said that his sons and the other disciples have returned from the trip the rabbi had sent them on. They are on a retreat to rest and report. So…I don't know…maybe they will all be together up there for several more days."

"All right! Thank you," Nathaniel said. Turning to Philip he added, "I must tell my crew we will not work tonight."

Philip asked, "Then we'll go to him tomorrow?"

Nathaniel, looking first at Elias then Philip, answered, "Yes. We will plan a trip for tomorrow."

Elias and Jacob nodded. Philip knew that he could not take his class with him on such a long trip. He asked the members of his family to contact the parents of the boys to cancel lessons for the next day. Jacob, now desiring to hear the man for himself, raised his voice to attract the attention of the people who were

187

visiting with one another. He announced the cancellation of all classes for the next morning. And Nathaniel lined up his crewmen to help carry Philip.

According to Mosaic Law, no labor could be performed on the Sabbath. During the afternoon Nathaniel and Elias "went for a walk." Actually, they scouted out where Y'shua was camped. It was an hour's walk following a footpath through ravines and gullies, gradually ascending into the hills east of Bethsaida. They found him surrounded, not only by his twelve disciples, but by a multitude of people! The rabbi was not teaching at that time, and the people were patiently waiting for the next time. Nathaniel was not surprised at finding the crowd, but Elias was amazed.

"I wonder if we'll be able to get Philip up to the rabbi through all these people," Elias thought out loud.

"I'm willing to make a try, if you are," Nathaniel replied.

"Oh, of course! It's good, though, that you have the crew standing by to help."

"They offered. They were with me when I listened to the rabbi preaching in the hills out of Capernaum…they want to hear more of what he has to say. Also, they remember Philip before he was paralyzed, and would like to have him able-bodied again."

"It will be wonderful to have him able to walk! Has the whole village turned into followers?"

"No. You have not noticed much decline in attendance at the synagogue, have you? Most of these people follow the rabbi from place to place, and they have come from all over the country."

They turned to retrace their steps.

The men were back in their home when the Sabbath ended. Plans were made to carry Philip out to the encampment. The whole family would make the trip, except Elizabeth, who was great with child, and Esther, Philip's youngest. The women were as aware of the importance of the trip as were the men. Not only did they hope to see Philip healed of his paralysis; if Y'shua were the Messiah, to have seen him with their own eyes would be an event to be told and re-told to their children and grandchildren. Each person, adult and child, would carry a bag of food—bread, dried fruit and cheese.

The crewmen from Nathaniel's fishing boat would help carry Philip's litter. Because of the discomfort Philip had experienced when he was taken to the seashore, Sapporo had made a pallet-size pillow for padding. She put loops on each corner to go over the ends of the rods, thereby keeping it in place while being carried. Philip had enjoyed its added softness ever since she presented it to him.

## Chapter Thirty-five

The next morning dawned clear of any clouds—a perfect day for a walk into the hills behind Bethsaida. The chill of early morning prompted each person to put on a cloak. The crewmen, their wives and children arrived just when the sun was rising over the hills into which they were going. Nathaniel and Elias positioned themselves at each end of Philip's bed, squatting down to pick it up. Jacob held open the courtyard door for them, and the men, children and women followed. One of the crewmen said, "Let us know when you want us to relieve you."

Nathaniel answered, "We will have to stop often for the children to rest, so we can alternate that way."

Philip, with emotion, said, "I want all of you to know how much I appreciate what you are doing. I praise Jehovah… "His voice broke, and in a slightly higher pitch finished, "…for family and friends like you."

Elias answered, "We want to see you walking again, dear brother."

So the party proceeded up the trail toward the encampment. It took twice as long as one able-bodied person could have made it. The crewmen alternated with Nathaniel and Elias about every twenty minutes.

They followed a creek bed up the ravine that now had a trickle of water in it. After about two hours they came upon the crowd of people who had camped with

Y'shua and his disciples. The center seemed to be near the spring that fed the creek. The ravine had broadened at that location. Trees and shrubbery were growing in an otherwise barren area. The people were on the hillsides that surrounded the oasis. Thousands of people! Many were ill and on litters. The party stopped at the edge of the crowd. No one seemed to notice that another group of people had joined the throng.

Philip sat up and said, "Oh! How are we ever going to get through this crowd! I think we made a big mistake." The nearest folk then turned to look at them.

Nathaniel said, "Worry not, big brother. We didn't bring you out here to become discouraged!"

Elias added, "If anyone can get you through, we can!"

The people shushed them. Distant voices could be heard, but they hadn't realized the people were listening. Elias whispered, "Sorry."

They all sat quietly on the ground where they were, and strained to hear words being uttered at the center of the multitude. The voices carried fairly well on the still morning air down the ravine. With concentration they could make out most of what was being said. It sounded like a confrontation between members of one of the religious sects and Y'shua about his healing on the Sabbath. They heard Y'shua say, "If your animal fell into a pit on a Sabbath, would you leave him there, or would you get help from your neighbors and pull him out?"

A voice answered, "That is different."

Y'shua, "How is it different? One of God's creatures gets into trouble, and you have the

191

ability…not only the ability, the responsibility…to help it. Do you not know that men and women are more important than animals? Look at all the sick people…if you could relieve their suffering, would you not do it?"

They heard no response. Nathaniel whispered to Philip, "I am going to look around to see if there is an opening anywhere," and stood up.

Elias, who had overheard, said, "I will go with you," and also arose to his feet, as did the two crewmen.

As the men moved around the edge of the crowd, everyone heard another voice say, "You allow your disciples to do labor on the Sabbath. That is against our Law."

Y'shua asked, "What are you talking about?"

"We observed them picking corn in a field, and eating it without first washing. First they did labor, and then they transgressed the Law again by not cleaning themselves."

"What do you do when you are hungry, if you are not fasting? Eat! Do you not remember reading about David, when he was hungry, taking the priest's holy food? He also gave it to those who were with him. No one but the priests was 'allowed' to eat that food. God made the Sabbath for humanity…not the other way around."

Y'shua continued, "As for eating without first washing…it is not what one puts into one's stomach, nor how clean his hands are, that is important, but what is in one's heart. If a person is a liar or cheater, the cleanest hands will not be of any use."

Silence ensued, except for quiet movement of the multitude. After a few moments, the buzz of conversation among the people started.

The men returned after about half an hour. Nathaniel told Philip, "This crowd is gathered so tightly that we can see only one possibility of getting you through."

"What is it?" Philip dubiously asked.

"We must go beyond the trees...the people are not so close together up there."

"Oh," he groaned, "That means carrying me up the hill to go around the crowd, doesn't it?" Philip asked.

"Yes...but we brought you this far. We want to do what has to be done to get you to Y'shua," Elias replied.

Philip sighed, "If you're sure that it will not be too much hard work."

Nathaniel said, "We are used to pulling in nets full of fish. You don't weigh as much as they do."

"Well, it's your backs and muscles. I'm ready if you are," Philip said, grinning.

The four men each took hold of Philip's pallet, and lifted him. Jacob, the women and children followed the litter party. The hillside on the south side of the spring had a gentler slope than the one on the north. So the group started climbing the rise. Dry grass crackled underfoot, as they made their way up the hill. They went around the crowd, to a place beyond the trees where the people were farther apart. They stopped to rest. The sun was getting higher in the sky and the day had warmed.

From this angle the heads of the men at the center of the encampment were visible. Before lowering

Philip's bed to the ground, he sat up on it and joined everyone in looking at Y'shua. He wasn't hard to pick out. He was wearing a white garment. Although his height was average, he seemed to stand taller than his companions. The sun reflected in the hair of his uncovered head. Philip remembered seeing him in the boat with the illusion of an aura extending beyond his head and body. He looked for the circle of light, and— yes, it was there again. He and his disciples were talking softly about some bread and fish in baskets. Only a syllable now and then carried to where they were.

Without a word, Jacob picked up Ruth, one of Philip's daughters. The men put the pallet on the ground and Elias lifted his son into his arms, as did the crewmen their smallest children. Nathaniel swooped up the twins, one in each arm. Mary reached out and placed her arms around the waists of the two women nearest her. Then those two women did the same with the other two. This was a moment to be etched in all their memories.

After a few minutes Jacob asked Ruth, "Are you hungry?"

"Yes!" came a chorus of answers from all the children as they were lowered to stand on their own feet.

"It made me hungry when he started talking about eating." He said a prayer, and each person sat on the ground, taking food from their bag and ate.

Elias said, "We don't have to worry that we can't wash our hands, according to what he said…we have to be concerned only that our hearts are clean."

Jacob said, "He has some revolutionary ideas, all right."

Philip was very interested in knowing his father's reaction to all that they had observed thus far. He was about to speak when someone called out, "Clear paths so we can give you some bread and fish."

Nathaniel looked at his crewmen and said, "Are we going to witness another miracle of feeding a multitude?" They shrugged, not knowing what to say.

The people began to move closer together to form space for someone to walk through. Y'shua held aloft a loaf of bread in one hand and a fish in the other, gave thanks to his "Father God," and broke the bread. He continued breaking the bread, a total of seven loaves. Nathaniel counted them. He didn't know how many fish, but there were not many, and they were small.

Soon one of the disciples brought a basket of bread and fish up the hill where they were seated. When offered, Jacob said, "Thank you, but we have brought food from our homes." The man said, "Most of these people have been here three days, and are out of food. Our master has great compassion for them."

"I can see that," Jacob replied.

About thirty minutes later, the disciples brought baskets around to collect the broken pieces that had been left over. Philip's party put in some from their own sacks. They watched as the collection was gathered, and the individual baskets were emptied into others. Seven baskets were filled!

Philip asked Nathaniel and Elias, "How many people do you think are in this crowd?"

They looked at each other. Elias said, "I estimate twelve thousand total."

Nathaniel nodded and said, "If our party is typical, the men are outnumbered two to one." Then he added, "I'm glad to have you folks witness this for yourselves. I know that you couldn't quite believe me when I told you what he did before."

Elias answered, "Yes. Even now it's difficult to understand, and I have seen it for myself."

Philip said, "Do you think this would be a good time to try to come close to him?"

Nathaniel answered, "This is an excellent time. I see a path right now." With that he stood and grabbed one end of the bed. Philip laid back. Elias stood and went to the other end. They picked it up together and started down the hill.

As though on cue, the multitude also stood to bring their sick ones to Y'shua. And, — he started to leave the camp!

The open path soon closed. Parents reached for the hands of children to keep them from being separated and lost in the crowd. Elias, who was leading the party, forged ahead. The others followed Nathaniel single file. They moved slowly down the hillside. As they went through the oasis, individually they felt as though they were walking on holy ground. The shade of the trees was refreshing. The very air seemed to have a different quality.

As Y'shua moved down the ravine, he stopped each time he saw a person in need of healing. Joyful sounds of praise resounded from the cured individuals as well as their loved ones. When Y'shua would halt, chain-reaction caused a stoppage of forward movement in the crowd that followed.

Communicating was difficult in this crowded condition, so Philip kept his thoughts to himself. He realized that they would never be able to catch up with Y'shua. At last, after about three hours, the crowd reached the seashore. Y'shua and his disciples had boarded a boat and were sailing away!

# Chapter Thirty-five

Philip's litter was put on the ground. The family gathered around him. Some of the crowd was doing the same as they were—watching the boat sail away. Others had started to follow on foot around the lake.

Philip said, "Nathaniel, if we were to get aboard your boat, would we get to the far shore before the crowd?"

"We could surely try!" He hesitated, and then hurriedly added, "But not all of us can get on board."

Mary, immediately understanding the situation, spoke, "We'll take the children and go home." Turning to the other women said, "Is that all right with you?"

They all agreed.

With an unusual public showing of affection, Mary came to Philip, knelt down, and put her arms around him. He responded by embracing her and kissing her on the cheeks. Tears were in the eyes of both as they released their embrace and looked at each other. She said, barely above a whisper, "I am so proud of you! You have not allowed this disappointment to kill your spirit." With that she stood and started to leave. The other women were not as brave as Mary, but each stopped by Philip's bed and gave him a sympathetic look of affection. He returned their looks, silently thanking them for their support and the sacrifice each was making on his behalf. He couldn't trust his voice to verbalize his thoughts.

With the women and children headed for their homes, Nathaniel and Elias lifted Philip on his pallet and carried him to the dock where their boat was tied. The crewmen jumped into the boat and brought it alongside the pier. Jacob climbed aboard.

The three men in the boat reached out to help transfer Philip into the boat. With everyone safely aboard, one of the crewmen untied the boat, the other unfurled the sails.

Other people from the crowd were doing likewise. A flotilla of boats would be racing across the sea that afternoon. A good race depends on wind, and, except for a slight onshore breeze that opposed their departure, the sea was calm that day!

The boat carried only one set of oars; the crewmen took the first turn in rowing the boat across the sea. Nathaniel and Elias alternated with them. Elias found that he had lost some of the strength he had when he was a fisherman, and he couldn't row as long as Nathaniel. So Jacob would take a turn to relieve Elias, and it had been years since Jacob had rowed a boat.

Meanwhile, the people on foot were moving faster than they were. They could see that the boats would be the losers in the race to the other side.

## Chapter Thirty-six

Mary and Sarah entered their courtyard. It was too quiet. All was not right. Mary called, "Elizabeth!" No answer.

Sarah dropped her cloak and food bag and ran up the stairs. Mary looked in the stable and garden area. Soon they met again in the courtyard. Elizabeth and Esther were not at home.

"Where could she be?" asked Sarah. "She is too big and near her confinement to go visiting."

"Could her term be due today?" Mary asked.

"She couldn't send Esther for the midwife...she is too young..."

Mary interrupted, "...so she took Esther and went to the midwife's!"

"Yes! That's exactly what she'd do. I'll go and find out."

"Thank you, daughter. I'll stay here with the children. We all need to rest...it's been a long day."

"Now, if she's there, I'll stay. So, if I don't return immediately, you'll know that's where she is. All right?"

"If you need me, will you come for me?"

"Zipporah lives near the midwife. I'll ask her to come for you. Is that all right?"

"That's a good plan. Go now, and God be with you."

As Sarah hurried the several streets to the midwife's, her thoughts went back to the last birth in their extended household, Esther, and the death of her mother, Hannah. *The happenings in our lives during the past two years started with that event. Elizabeth is a healthy, mature woman—she shouldn't have any trouble.*

Inasmuch as Zipporah's house came before the midwife's, Sarah decided to stop there first, just in case that was where Elizabeth had gone. She rapped and then opened the courtyard door. Zipporah and her husband were seated at the table. Zipporah jumped to her feet and ran to embrace Sarah. Instantly realizing something was distressing her, Zipporah asked, "What's wrong?"

"I'm looking for Elizabeth. I can see that she's not here," and turned to leave.

"No, we haven't seen her today."

Half turning back, Sarah said, "I'm on my way to the midwife's, and decided to stop in the event she was here."

"I'll go with you to the midwife's. I may be needed."

They left the courtyard. Sarah recounted briefly the day's events as they walked the remaining distance to the home of the midwife. As they entered the courtyard, Sarah breathed a prayer to Jehovah to give them a fully developed, strong baby and a safe birthing for Elizabeth.

Esther was sleeping on a pallet on the floor in the courtyard. Sarah called, "Elizabeth! Keziah! It's Sarah and Zipporah," and headed up the stairs.

"We're up here," replied Keziah, the midwife. As Sarah and Zipporah entered the room, Keziah said, "I'm glad you've come. We could use some help."

Elizabeth was seated on the birth stool—two padded stones that supported the mother in a squatting position. She looked at Sarah and Zipporah and smiled faintly. Her face showed the strain of having suffered the pangs of giving birth.

"Here comes another one!" Elizabeth cried out.

"Sarah, go behind her and give her a hand." Pulling up her garments, Sarah sat down directly behind Elizabeth, one leg on each side of the birth stool, put her arms under Elizabeth's arms, placed her hands on the abdomen and pushed. When the pain momentarily subsided, Elizabeth relaxed against Sarah's body for support.

Keziah said, "The pains are almost constant now, so it shouldn't be too long. Zipporah, will you bring some warm water? We have two jars up here, but they're cold."

"All right." Zipporah said, and left to go to the courtyard below, where a basin of water on top of the oven was being heated.

"Now, Elizabeth," Keziah said firmly but softly, "I want you to push just as hard as you can. Bear down on that little fellow."

"Yes, 'Mother' Keziah. I'll push hard. Oh!" she groaned.

"Push! Push! Push! I see his head! You are doing great. Keep pushing."

Elizabeth leaned back against Sarah from fatigue. But just for a moment. She groaned and tensed her body to help her little one enter the world. Just as

Zipporah returned with warm water, the baby issued forth.

"It's a boy!" Keziah called out, "A beautiful, healthy baby boy."

"Praise God," was uttered by all three women.

Keziah slapped the baby on his backside, forcing out the mucus that was in his nose and mouth, and he bellowed forth his first cry. She used her copper knife to cut the umbilical cord, and tied it before handing him to Zipporah to wash. She finished the birthing procedures, washing and padding Elizabeth, and took away the birth stool. Sarah moved away so Elizabeth could lie back and rest.

After the baby was bathed, his body was rubbed with oil and salt. Then swaddling cloths—long strips of woolen fabric—were wrapped tightly around his legs, arms and body so he would have straight limbs.

Elizabeth, smiling, observed everything. As the newborn was placed in her arms she said, "Nathaniel will be so happy."Then she wanted to know from Sarah what had happened out in the hills. Sarah briefly summarized the day's events.

Keziah said, "Elizabeth, I'd like you to stay overnight here. Tomorrow will be soon enough for you to return home. And, remember, you are unclean for forty days. It's my duty as a midwife to remind you that you must not appear in public places." Then, laughing, she said, "I think your husband will not want you to stay with me for forty days, though."

"All right, Keziah, for over night."

"We'll go now, and let you rest. Mother Mary will be anxious to know about you." Sarah and Zipporah each leaned over Elizabeth, caressing her cheek, and departed. They took Esther with them as far as Zipporah's. She was as much at home there as at Jacob's home.

# Chapter Thirty-seven

As the boats approached the shore at Capernaum, the breeze filled their sails to help them reach the dock. It gave the men a brief respite before beginning the task of carrying Philip to locate Y'shua. They had no doubt they would find him—wherever the crowd was, he would be in the center.

The boat was tied to a pier. Philip and his bed were lifted out. Each man, except Jacob, took an end. Elias and Nathaniel shared the load at Philip's feet and led the way. Jacob walked beside Philip. Up the incline of the beach they went, falling in with the people who had come on foot.

They didn't know where they were going; they just followed the crowd. They had faith they would be led to Y'shua and this time they would carry Philip right up to the Master, and there—Philip would be healed. What they didn't know was the series of obstacles they were about to encounter.

They turned into a residential neighborhood. The forward movement halted.

The homes were typical of the villages in the area of the Sea of Galilee: flat roofed, one and two-story mud-brick houses, some with enclosed courtyards like Jacob's, some without. Second and third stories were built when a family expanded and more rooms were needed. The second floor and roofs were accessible by either an outside stair such as in Jacob's house, or ladders.

Roofs were used for a multiple of purposes: drying clothes, fruits and vegetables, privacy, dining after a very hot day, sleeping during hot weather, and meditation, to name a few. A wall of about eighteen inches protected children and objects from falling off.

The crowd surrounding the homes was so large it was hard for Philip's party to ascertain exactly which house was the center of attention. The houses were close together. They were built that way for mutual protection in time of war; also, it gave the homeowners a larger area for all their gardens to be in one spot.

Philip said, "Nathaniel, it may be wise for you to scout ahead and find out which house he's in. What do you think?"

Nathaniel answered, "Yes. I've been thinking the same thing. I'll look around."

They put Philip down and Nathaniel left, trying to squirm his way through the body of people packed around them.

After about half an hour Nathaniel returned and said, "He's supposed to be in that house two doors down the street. I came close enough to see that it has no courtyard wall, so he must be in a room inside the house. It's going to be difficult to get through the press of people, carrying this litter."

Philip said, "Are the people packed this tightly on the other side of the house?"

Nathaniel said, "No, they're not!" As though reading Philip's thoughts, added, "That's what we'll do…take you by way of another street, and come in from the other way!"

So the men picked up Philip's bed and backtracked to where they could go above the street the house was on. People were there, too, but not as many. Then they paralleled, as much as they could, the street where they had been, until they were beyond the house they were headed for. They turned down and approached the house from the other side. Nathaniel was right: the people were not as many, but still numerous.

As they approached the open courtyard, the crowd formed a solid wall. One of the crewmen, who was in the lead at the time, said to the people ahead of them, "We want to bring our friend to Y'shua for healing. Please let us through."

The folks close to them tried to step back to make space for them, but had no room. "Sorry," one of them said.

The litter party retreated to the edge of the multitude. As they put Philip's pallet down, they all seated themselves on the ground. Elias asked, "What shall we do?"

Nathaniel said, "We have to do something. We didn't come here for another disappointment. Does anyone have any suggestions?"

They were silent for a moment, sizing up the situation. Finally Jacob said, "Perhaps we should just give up. It's been a long day, and all of you must be tired…I know I am!"

Suddenly Philip excitedly pointed toward the house and said, "Look! An outside stairway to the roof!"

All heads turned in the direction he indicated. This was a one-story house. Elias voiced what the rest were thinking, "So we can go to the roof. What good is that?"

The roofs were constructed with rafters, placed two to three feet apart, over which were laid brushwood branches woven together. Mud of clay was then spread to fill the cracks. It hardened to form a smooth plaster. Each year the homeowner had to repair and maintain his roof. He had a weighted roller that he pulled to force the mud into the crevices of the branches and to leave a smooth finish.

Nathaniel said, "What do you have in mind, Philip?"

"Well," Philip said slowly, "Since this is summertime, I doubt the roof has been made ready for the winter rains…"

Nathaniel finished his thought, "…and we can cut a hole and lower you through the roof! What a great idea!"

A possible solution to their problem invigorated each of their tired bodies. They started to stand, each fisherman feeling for his knife. Philip said, "What will you need?"

Nathaniel said, "We could use a rope. You can hang on to the poles of your bed, but you may not be able to hold on long enough, and you would slide off."

Elias, now as enthused as the others, added, "Yes, we need two ropes, one at each end of his litter."

Jacob, caught up in the challenge contributed, "You cut a hole big enough for the litter, put the ropes at each end, as Elias just said, and lower him with the ropes. Good plan!"

One of the crewmen said, "I'll go to the boat for ropes and extra knives." He departed, weaving his way through the crowd. Meanwhile, the four men carried Philip up the stairs to the roof of the house.

It was late afternoon of a warm day, and the roof was hot. The view gave them a perspective of the multitude they had been a part of. The whole village looked like an anthill—more people were still arriving from around the lake, and others were coming from houses and shops. The serenity of the calm lake reflecting the clear blueness of the sky, contrasted against the ageless brown hills surrounding it, gave the viewers a sense of their purpose.

"We must be careful where we step...we don't want to fall through before we accomplish what we've set out to do," said Jacob.

Nathaniel said, "I'll start to make small holes to determine the area where we want to enlarge one big enough to lower him through it." And he carefully stepped to feel for the security of a rafter underfoot, knelt and started plunging his fishing knife into the plaster and brush. The other crewman followed suit in another location. Neither Elias nor Jacob had a knife with them.

On the crewman's second hole, he said, "He is below here. I can see someone talking to him."

Nathaniel stood and carefully joined the crewman, knelt and peered through the peephole. "Yes, this is the place."

Now the two of them began to enlarge the hole, kneeling on rafters on each side of it. Soon the other crewman returned with ropes and knives. He put down the ropes, and handed Elias and Jacob each a knife. Taking his own knife he and the other two carefully stepped to the area where the hole was being made. The group began to work in earnest to enlarge it big enough.

To avoid debris from dropping through the hole, they were careful to grasp a handful before cutting or breaking it off.

It wasn't long before they were the center of attention of those in the room below. Everyone was watching as the hole became bigger and bigger. Of course, some plaster dust and twigs did fall through despite the care they were taking.

Now came the big move: to get the ropes under Philip's bed and gently lower him on it over the opening.

Ropes were placed across the opening, dividing it into thirds. Elias and Jacob held one each on the far side. A crewman was ready to pick up both on the near side.

Nathaniel and the other crewman picked up Philip and carried him to the opening. They balanced themselves with one foot on the rafters on each side of it. When the litter was in place over the opening and the ropes, the crewman then quickly picked up the two ropes.

Nathaniel carefully lowered his end of the pallet, feeling for the tension the ropes were to provide. He took one of the two ropes his crewman held. The men leaned backward pulling the ropes taut to keep Philip from falling through too soon.

The weight of the other end was released to the support of the ropes. The crewman then took the rope Jacob was holding.

Philip was now being suspended in the opening. Sighs of relief escaped, as they realized their plan was going to work. It was just a matter now of carefully feeding rope, and allowing Philip's weight to pull him downward.

Philip had been a quiet observer as his brothers, father and friends worked to accomplish this feat. The pressure of the ropes under his pallet gave him assurance he wouldn't fall. He felt excitement building for there was no doubt now that at last he was going to reach Y'shua.

The intense heat of many bodies on a warm day was momentarily noticed as he was lowered into the room. His heart thumped in his chest, and his breath became shallow. What is Y'shua thinking?

Space had been made in the room for him. In fact, the people had moved away from under the opening to avoid the falling debris, and to observe the entire operation.

As Philip reached a level that he could see heads of those standing, he first saw some scribes. He knew them by the reed symbol that he had worn. However, he did not know them personally. Among others in the room were Simon and Andrew who recognized him, but they said nothing.

Then his eyes found those of Y'shua. They were intent on him—he had not remembered them as being so commanding at Qumran. Did Y'shua remember him? As though in answer to his unvoiced question came the vision of Y'shua in his dream. Yes, he felt assured Y'shua remembered him. The intense blue eyes told Philip this is the day we both have been waiting for. This day will further the work for the kingdom of heaven.

When Philip felt the earthen floor beneath him, he sat up on his pallet, and opened his mouth to speak.

Instead, he heard the kindest voice say, "My son, your sins are forgiven."

A sense of an intense love swept through his body.

Shocked silence engulfed the room. He stared at Y'shua, puzzling *what exactly did he mean.*

Involuntarily, because of lifelong training and teaching, Philip's immediate reaction was: *only God can forgive sins.* But he caught himself from thinking any further, *because if this man truly is the Messiah, he would have the power to forgive sins.*

As if Y'shua had read his mind, although he addressed the scribes, who must have been thinking the same way as Philip, with a tone that indicated *why are you challenging my authority* he said, "Why do you question? Is it not easier to say, 'Your sins are forgiven' than it is to say, 'Rise, take up your bed and walk'?"

Philip couldn't grasp that forgiving his sins would enable him to walk. He asked himself: *what sins have I committed that need forgiving?*

In an instant he was flooded with a sense of grief from the death of his beloved wife, Hannah, and the blame he placed on himself for it. Not only Hannah's death, but that of her father, too. Y'shua had said, "Your sins are forgiven!" At that moment he recognized relief and release from the burden of those terrible guilty feelings. He started to weep with joy. As though a floodgate had opened with this knowledge, he felt strength returning to his lower limbs. Praise Jehovah! I have been healed!

Meanwhile, Y'shua was saying in no uncertain terms to the scribes, "So you may know that I, as the son of man, have the authority to forgive sins, ..." he turned to Philip and said, "Rise, take up your pallet and go home."

Philip sat there, astounded at what had happened to him. He had expected to be healed, but hadn't given thought as to how to actually start walking again. It had been a long time since he had been able to support himself on his own legs, but he intended to do as Y'shua commanded or his best in trying.

He had to bend his knees. Out of habit he reached down to pull his legs up, at the same time wishing they would respond. Yes! They obeyed his mental direction. He brought his legs and feet up under him as far as he could. *Oh! How marvelous to have them do what he wanted them to.*

Turning to one side, he rolled over into a kneeling position, knees on the floor beside his pallet and his feet still on it. Praise the Lord! *Now, if those legs will just bear my weight, I'll be able to stand.* He brought his right knee up so his foot was on the floor. Reaching upward with his right hand, it was met by a strong hand belonging to one of the scribes. With that leverage and pushing against the floor with the other hand, Philip rose to a standing position.

Applause and loud praise erupted from everyone in the room. He looked up through the hole in the roof. Though his vision was blurred, he could see the faces of his loved ones beaming down on him, their tears flowing. *They have witnessed this miracle, praise God! Praise God!*

They in turn saw an upturned face glowing with happiness, along with the tears streaming down his face.

*Will I be able to walk? First I must pick up my bed.* As he again bent his knees to lower his body to do so, he heard someone in the crowd say, "We've never seen anything like this before!"

The rest responded, "Glory to God!"

Philip wondered if it would be any easier to get through this crowd going out than it was trying to get in. He tucked his bed under one arm and went out the door. *I am walking! ...walking!...walking! I am actually putting one foot in front of the other and staying upright! Praise Jehovah! Oh! What a magnificent feeling. I am tingling all over.*

The crowd outside the door had watched as the men had carried Philip up the stairs. When Philip appeared carrying his pallet, praises to God could be heard and the clapping of hands. The men hurried down from the roof and met Philip, embracing and kissing him on each cheek.

To them Philip repeated, "He said, 'Rise, take up your bed and go home.' I must complete his command, and go home...but I will follow that man wherever he leads me! I will serve him for the rest of my life. He is the Messiah. I know it! I know it. I know it. My entire being tells me it is so!"

"Yes, Philip, we know it, too," his father replied.

# # #

# ABOUT THE AUTHOR

Vada McRae Gipson is the daughter of a Circuit Rider in western Nebraska of the Free Methodist Church (before she was born).

Today, she is an active member of the United Methodist Church. She is retired from McDonnell Douglas Corporation (now Boeing Corporation) as an accountant, and is a freelance writer.

A reading of *The Dead Sea Scrolls 1947-1969* by Edmund Wilson captivated her imagination and inspired the writing of this, her first book. It is the result of her fascination with the Essene Sect, members of which may have been the inhabitants of Qumran, the "tel" that is located near where the Dead Sea Scrolls were found. The story is fiction based on six years of research.

She feels that she received blessings to enable her to write the book (and surprised herself!). May it in turn be a blessing to the reader.

Printed in the United States
853000002B

9 781403 364258